THINK LIKE A BANK

A powerful financial self-help book that can
help you transform your quality of life just
by re-educating your mind

By
Norma Cassius

Published by
Norma Cassius
96 Harley Street, London W1G 7HY
United Kingdom
www.normacassius.com
Telephone +44 (0)7845891035

Think Like a Bank
Book by Norma Cassius
Copyright © 2019 Norma Cassius
ISBN 978-1-5136-4415-8
Printed 2019

Dedication

This book is dedicated to my late parents, Birchell and Dorrel Murray. Their different styles of money management practices have played an integral part in my financial success. I am sure they would be somewhat surprised to hear this, because when they thought I was not listening to their advice I was paying full attention. To this end, I thank them from the bottom of my heart for being so instrumental in helping me become financially savvy – a skill which has helped me have the quality of life I possess today.

TABLE OF CONTENTS

Preface   vii

Introduction   1

Chapter 1:   Know the Rules   4

Chapter 2:   The Psychology of Debt   37

Chapter 3:   5 Golden Financial Educational Nuggets   54

Chapter 4:   Facing Money Problems   81

Chapter 5:   Never Too Young to Start   89

Chapter 6:   Budgeting the Smart Way   103

Chapter 7:   Having an Idea Can Make
                    You a Millionaire!   114

Chapter 8:   Now Start Setting Your Goals   126

Acknowledgements   146

To The Reader   148

Appendix   151

Useful Websites for Good Deals   153

Comparison Websites   154

Free Banking Apps   155

Consultation   157

Preface

There are a couple of reasons I felt led to title my book *'Think like a Bank'*. Firstly, I was aways frustrated and unhappy about living on the bread line. I worked for banks' for over two decades, and while I struggled financially, they continued to make lots of money. After much deliberation, I realised that I could do what banks' do for myself. This is what I do to this day.

I wanted to live a life where I was in control of my finances as opposed to my finances being in control of me. A large percentage of people today have settled for a life whereby they live from month to month depending on their salary. Like me at one point, most people's salaries are probably already accounted for by the time it is paid into our account. If this sounds very close to home and is where you are today, I am sure you will agree that this is a life of existing, as opposed to real living.

Secondly, *'Think Like a Bank'* is all about playing a game which requires thinking smart and being smart. I am here to show you how to do that by using banks' principles to benefit you. My goal is to equip you to beat banks' at their own game by making better financial choices.

Consider this book your money management manual. Like an instruction manual that guides you through a product you purchased so you can maximise its fullest potential. This book will help you maximise your money to its fullest potential. It will also guide you into becoming your own Personal Money Management Adviser (PMMA). Once you have mastered the rules and strategies of this manual, you can then begin to apply them to your finances. You will eventually start noticing positive results, and when that happens, you can confidently add the title 'PMMA' after your name!

Introduction

Allow me to introduce myself. I'm Norma Cassius, a money management consultant with over 20 years of working within the financial sector and a qualified psychotherapist with over 15 years' experience.

I have worked in many financial and clinical settings, and found many people like myself who wished they could find solutions to their money problems. They seem to be at a loss as to which way to turn. If I were given a pound every time I told someone I was a money management consultant, I would be a millionaire by now! They usually respond by either saying, "I need help with my money," or "You need to help me".

Do you feel you could use a little help too? Do you ever ask yourself the following questions?

1. What would my quality of life look like if I made the most out of my money?
2. Why am I working harder than ever, earning more but still not making ends meet?
3. How do I start making smart financial choices?
4. I am in debt - how do I dig my way out of it?

If you wonder about any of the above, this book is for you.

It will help you get started on your journey to becoming financially savvy!

I am aware that money can be such a sensitive and personal subject matter. I find that some people seem to plod along in agony, keeping their financial problems close to their chest instead of seeking help and support. You do not have to be embarrassed about experiencing financial challenges any longer. 'Think Like a Bank' is here to help! I am shouting from the roof top that you do not have to live this way.

This financial self-help book is packed with a collection of insightful examples and facts about financial institutions' practices. I have also combined some of my personal financial experiences to give you a well-rounded book.

My primary objective is to attempt to convey some of the banks' successful strategies and tweak them to make it work for you. These strategies will help you become skilled in managing and maximising your finances. Whether you are earning a regular salary, a budding entrepreneur or planning your retirement, you will be inspired to put some of these examples into action right away!

While reading this book, you will notice that I use powerful quotes and analogies to emphasise some of the information I share. I find communicating in this way is quite effective at getting the point across. So, I will start the book with the first quote:

"No matter the economy of the jungle,
Lions will never eat grass".

Lions have standards,and so should we. Life does not have to be about just paying bills and struggling to make ends meet. There must be a better way to live, and that is what I endeavour to show you.

CHAPTER 1

Know the Rules

Are you ready to *think like a bank*? If the answer is yes, then you will need the rules of this financial game to get you started. In any game, you have to be "in it to win it". To ensure you are on the winning side, applying the rules to receive all the benefits is essential. With great knowledge comes great success and power.

The game we are playing is the 'money management game' where banks' and financial institutions originally wrote the rules for their benefit. However, financial institutions had to change their policies (since the financial crisis in 2008,) whereby banks' were encouraged to become more customer-focused when selling their financial products.

You will need to be very clear about the rules when you are playing your part in the game so you can reap the financial successes you deserve. This will now be possible because you will be playing the game by the banks' rules.

After reading this chapter, you should be enthusiastic and empowered to start thinking about what steps to take. Buckle up; you are in for an exciting ride that will take you to a place in your mind you may never have thought possible.

The functions of banks

Let's look at a brief overview of banks' functions, so you are clear about what they do:

Banks' and financial institutions offer a variety of different financial services and products (i.e. loans, mortgages, credit cards, savings and investment products) to individuals and businesses.

Banks' take customers' deposits in return for paying them an annual interest payment. The banks' then use most of these deposits to lend to other customers and institutions for a range of financial products as mentioned.

The banking system also helps channel funds from savers to borrowers in an efficient manner. Banks' play a fundamental role as a go-between in the financial system. They have three main functions:

1. People can safely deposit their savings
2. Banks' pay interest on deposited savings
3. They issue loans to both people and businesses

To win in this game, you need to have the Three S's: Strategy, Structure, which results in Success. Now let us look at the three S's.

STRUCTURE – Identify the areas you are financially challenged

Once identified, address each area by using the appropriate information shared in this book. I.e. switching to 0% financial products or having a highly detailed budget.

STRATEGY – Plan your action

When armed with the information about what you need to do in a particular area, take the first step and apply what you have learnt. Continue to apply the steps and actions until you accomplish your desired goal.

SUCCESS – You are in control of your money

To get to this point you would have successfully applied all the steps and actions to each challenging area of your finances. Hopefully, you are experiencing positive results and maximising your money to its full potential. Well done!

Being in the know

Knowing banks' winning strategies and implementing them is key to starting a new approach with managing your money. In other words, you aim to learn what banks' do then apply it to benefit you (knowledge is power).

Let's begin with one of their winning strategies that can

now become yours! Say you need to make a large purchase, such as a piece of furniture, but prefer not to use your own money or savings. You could obtain one of the bank's 0% credit cards that has anything from twelve to thirty-six months of interest-free credit (and pay it back within the agreed timescale, to purchase what you need).

What you have done is kept your savings, to invest or use elsewhere, used the banks' money at no extra costs to you (i.e. 0% credit card = no added interest), and have one to three years to pay it off.

Now, I completely understand that some people have finances saved for these types of purchases and avoid the idea of any credit at all. They would prefer to use their own money to buy what they need, and that is perfectly fine. However, I have taken this one step further to increase and maximise what I have, so let us take a look at the action I took.

A good few years ago, I wanted to decorate my living room, but I was reluctant to spend some of my savings to do this because I knew it would come to a tidy sum. After some thought about how I could achieve this and keep my savings intact, I saw an advert on TV advertising a credit card. The credit card had an extortionate APR (annual percentage rate) of 39.9%. For some reason, this prompted me to look in my purse and cast my eyes on my 0% credit card. Bingo! My 0% credit card was the answer. Well, it did not take me any time at all to furnish my whole living room without touching a penny of my savings, I paid back what I borrowed within the 24-month agreed timescale.

There was now an opportunity for me to put my savings to good use. I have always vowed that I would never keep a mortgage for the original contractual term of 25 years. Working in the financial sector, I knew how much money banks' were making on mortgage interest. This was the reason I strongly felt that I needed a way to pay off my mortgage sooner rather than later.

Make your move

I was ready to make my move. I used my savings to make overpayments on my mortgage. Doing this decreased its 25-year term and saved me thousands of pounds in interest. My 25-year mortgage was paid off in ten years.

Right there, I maximised my money by saving thousands of pounds. That is what I call being financially savvy. I did what banks' do (use our money to benefit themselves), well, I am now smart enough to use their money to benefit myself. This is how one of their win/win strategies can work for you. You are using their rules in your own 'financial game plan'. Banks' are successful and remain successful because they are experts at their game. If you follow these fundamental rules you can become successful too.

Example

Mortgage	Interest rate	Monthly repayment	Term
£150,000	5.39%	£912	25 yrs
£150,000	5.39%	£962 (extra £50)	22 yrs 6 months
£150,000	5.39%	£1,012 (extra £100)	20 yrs 5 months

(Figure 1)

The example shows the savings and the reduced term on a 25-year £150.000 mortgage by making overpayments:

Paying £50 extra a month would reduce the term to 22 years and six months with a savings of £14,534 in interest alone.

Paying £100 extra a month would reduce the term to 20 years and five months with a savings of £25,817 in interest alone.

The savvy thing to do here (if possible) is to make monthly overpayments. The more you can overpay, the more thousands of pounds, you will save in interest, and the faster you will pay off your mortgage.

This Information is taken from Moneysavingexpert.com – "mortgage overpayment calculator" – (accessed 21 April, 2018)

N.B. please ensure that you check with your bank or other financial providers that hold your mortgage to determine the total amount of overpayments you can make per year. Most banks' have limitations and restrictions. If you want to overpay more than their agreed limit, there may be a penalty, which might not work out cost- effective for you.

Why do you think that is? Obviously, it is not in their best interest for people to pay off their loans earlier than the agreed contractual term. They would lose out on thousands of pounds in interest, the money that we should have in our pockets!

You can see how real and doable this is. I have just used an example of overpaying £50 and £100. Evidently the more you overpay, the more you save and the earlier you pay off your mortgage.

Some people spend this amount on a night out or on a purchase. Such as the latest phone or an outfit. Now I am not saying do not treat yourself, because that would mean I am not being honest with you (I am forever having treats, whether it is to a spa or buying something new). Nonetheless, I just want to highlight the benefits of making overpayments.

For example, if you spend £100 a week or a month on socialising and buying clothes etc., maybe you could spend £50 on doing that and the other £50 on the overpayment of your mortgage or loan/debt. Right there you are getting the best of both worlds – it is a win/win situation.

Take it from me; once you start seeing the difference your overpayments are making on your mortgage statements, you will want to increase the amount you are overpaying. I got to a point where I regularly checked my monthly expenses to see what I could shave off.

Whatever savings I found, I would take that money to add to my overpayments. (This 'money management game' has become an exciting challenge). There are many ways to be savvy with your money, and I was becoming an expert! I am now in a financial position to reward myself for the savings I make. That did not happen overnight. Nevertheless, I can do it now, and so will you.

Once you have worked out how much you can overpay on any form of credit/debt, whether it is a credit or store card, loan or mortgage, implement this by first discussing it with the financial institution you have the product with – the bank or credit card company etc.

Find out their policy on overpayments as mentioned. Then amend your standing order or direct debit payments to reflect the new amount. What you have done is taken the first step to start the ball rolling in maximising and managing your money. (Well done!). Do not worry about how large or small your overpayments are. The key rule here is to try to overpay something. This will act as a trump card, from the example, the benefits are clear to see. Isn't that great? You are now on your way to earning your new title of a **P**ersonal **M**oney **M**anagement **A**dviser (PMMA)!

The savvy strategy here is to start by overpaying more on the loan/debts and less on your treats. When you have tipped the scales, and the loan is considerably less you should vividly see the savings you have made. Then and only then, you can begin to re-evaluate your treats. This is one of the ways you can guarantee saving yourself significant amounts of money, which in turn can help you become debt-free sooner rather than later.

Enjoy where you are on the way to where you are going

An important point to remember is to have some fun while playing the game. (Isn't that the reason we play games?). Saving £££s should put a smile on everyone's face leaving a sweet taste in your mouth.

Why? Because you have now found a way to help you have a win/win situation with your finances. That is overpayments that save you money in the long run by; 'saved amounts of interest' that in turn free up money for you to invest as well as spend some on yourself. Wow, how great is that!

The beauty of taking this action in the game is that it only took some tweaking with your finances. It did not require huge sacrifices, and boom! The fantastic result is, your finances and quality of life will eventually improve.

As previously mentioned, your mindset is key. There is a slogan about drink driving that goes. "Think before you drink, think twice before you drive". My slogan about maximising money goes like this, "Financial knowledge triggers actions, and actions result in financial success".

I really want to highlight that there are no savings account that can give you this type of return or savings you will make on your money. Meaning, the money you have saved by paying less on interest because of your overpayments which reduced the term (number of years on your loan.) The only thing that might give you this type of return is investing in stocks and shares, etc. However, it is advisable to have a Financial Adviser if you are considering this as there is some level of risk involved.

Credit

Some people think that not having any credit is a good thing. However, this attitude could work against you if you require a large purchase that is not affordable, like a mortgage. Not having enough information on your credit report/history is equally as bad as not paying your credit cards, loans and bills on time.

A credit report is a record of a borrowers' responsible repayment of debts. Places that loan money, like banks', and credit card companies use your credit report when deciding what you can borrow. Your credit report is so important that without a satisfactory one, you are unable to get a mortgage.

Another important fact, banks' do not like to see you paying the minimum amount on all your credit products. This could indicate that you are struggling financially. They believe they have us where they want, and for a large percentage of us they do.

I know there was a big taboo around accessing credit (credit/store cards and loans, etc.), namely how easy it was to obtain it previously. About a decade ago it was not unusual for credit to be offered to numerous people without them having to ask for it. That resulted in many people accumulating serious amounts of debt. This is what caused bad publicity because people were able to take out credit without the **knowledge** of how to use it. Banks' were not providing the sufficient knowledge required before the financial crisis in 2008, as mentioned previously.

For the financially vulnerable (the degree to which a person is capable of being injured financially when an unexpected event happens such as a job loss), being given credit in this way may have felt good to have access to the amounts of money that was offered. The financial institutions were probably sitting back with a smile on their faces because they knew these people were more than likely to spend all they were given. Moreover, they would now have to pay it back at an extortionate rate of interest.

Whose credit – the banks' or yours?

For most of my life, I had never earned a high salary, so I knew I had to be very practical and realistic with my money. I stayed away from purchasing anything on credit, and I did not own any cards, not even a cash card until I was about 33.

Everything was paid for by cash. I am quite old-fashioned, and I believe if you want something you cannot afford then you need to save for it. For me, it felt so good when I was actually able to purchase the item I had been saving for.

However, financially savvy people, successful business people and the wealthy know how to work the system. When they have an idea to buy a bank, bring out a new credit card, or take over a company, do you think they wait to save up X amount to do that, which will take X number of years? No way! For the majority of these people, their credit history is in good shape'. So they use the banks' money to make their purchases and pay it back within good time, so they pay minimal interest.

P Collinson, 'Half of UK adults are financially vulnerable' This information is taken from, The Guardian, 18 Oct 2017, (accessed 16 Dec, 2017).

If the amount they borrow is substantial and they have to pay interest on what they have borrowed, believe me, it won't be anything that will keep them financially stuck. They are more than likely able to negotiate a reasonable interest rate from the offset that benefits both themselves and the bank they are borrowing from.

Financial institutions have mastered the idea of using our deposited savings (DS) to gain significant profit when lending that same amount to others. In other words, if you deposited £2,000 in an account, banks' pay minimal interest of let us say 1-2%.

However, if you were to borrow £2,000 from a bank, you could be looking at an interest rate of anything from 3%-24.9% Depositing money is one thing but to borrow it, is entirely another.

We pay back extortionate amounts for what we have borrowed. Again, the rule in the game here is, do not unnecessarily give the banks' any of your hard-earned cash. You could save thousands if you transfer an outstanding credit card bal-

This Information is taken from "Santander, Personal Loans, information and rates." – (accessed 18 Aug, 2018)

ance with high interest to a 0% interest card (providing your credit history is ok).

Shop around on the comparison websites like moneysavingsexpert.com or comparethemarket.com. There are some excellent deals out there, and as mentioned earlier they have some offers of 0% cards from 12-36 months of free credit.

Please note, shop around for another 0% credit card and transfer your balance over to that before your deal expires. This action is only required if you are unable to pay off the outstanding balance within the agreed timescale.

Be aware! Most financial institutions charge a one-off transfer fee that will differ from bank to bank. Look for the cheapest transfer fee with the best 0% offer, meaning the credit card that is offering the best extended term, which can be anything up to 36 months.

Having said that, I have since found out that MBNA and Santander have a no balance transfer fee. Wow, this is even better! There may be other banks' that offer this as well, so shopping around is a fundamental rule in this game.

Example

(Santander 18.9% APR Credit Card with a £2,000 balance)

Repaying fixed amount	Credit card interest rate	Time taken to repay in full	Interest cost
£50.00/month	18.9% APR	5 years and 1 month	£1,017

(Figure 2)

The table above shows the time it takes to repay in full a credit card with a balance of £2,000 (five years and one month) with an interest rate of 18.9% APR. The total amount to repay, including interest of (£1,017) is £3,017.

This Information is taken from Moneysavingexpert.com – "minimum payment credit card calculator" – (accessed 18 April, 2018)

(MBNA Platinum 36 month 0% Credit Card Assuming You Make a Balance Transfer of £2,000)

Repaying fixed amount	Credit card interest rate	Balance transfer fee	Time taken to repay in full	Total cost of debt and fees
£56.66/month	0%	1.99%	3 years	£2,039.80
		1.99% of £2,000 is £39.80		

(Figure 3)

The MBNA table shows that it will take three years to repay in full a credit card with a balance of £2,000 (two years less than the Santander 18.9% APR credit card.) The one-off balance transfer fee is £39.80, so the total amount to repay is £2,039.80, saving you an alarming £977.20; what a win/win situation!

Again, can you see how banks' make their money? Nevertheless more importantly, can you see how you can start saving yours?

This information is taken from Uswitch.com – "balance transfer credit cards." – (accessed 18 April, 2018.)

If you do not have a 0% credit card and you are *not* paying your outstanding balance off each month in full, the interest you pay gets compounded to outrageous amounts the longer you are in debt. I will be discussing compound interest in the next chapter.

If we all began to use credit cards in the way I have just described, how could banks make their money? The truth of the matter is they have used us for long enough. They pay minimal interest on our savings between 1% and 2%.

Banks' use our money to reinvest while maximising their profit. Well, it is time that we start using their money to do the same. You need to start considering that this is possible and achievable; this is the mindset you need to adopt.

Now, I am aware that I have talked about people who have good credit. I am sure some of you may be thinking, 'my credit rating is not in a great place. How can this help me'? Well, the good news is if your finances are not in the best shape right now, that is ok. Setting some financial goals will help with this process. For example, mastering the necessary skills and techniques I will be sharing; which include. Cancelling all credit cards with credit on them that you are not using, Keeping your balances low on credit cards and making your payments on time. Throughout this book, you will also find more information which you can apply to boost your credit rating.

Putting these steps into action will help you work on a financial plan to improve your credit rating as well as maximise your money. For some people, additional help and support may be required, which will be the money management consultation I offer at my website www.normacassius.com. Further contact details are in the appendix.

The question I can see some of you asking yourself is "where do I start"? Well, the first step is changing your mindset. Once you know what you need to do, you must believe that it is possible. A famous Einstein quote is "Education is not the learning of facts; it's rather the training of the mind to think." Another unknown quote is "Even if education is free, a rat will never go to the same school as a cat." These quotes are about thinking smart and being smart.

Let's look at a few things to get you started:

1. Stop giving your money away. Would you go into a shop and purchase something that cost £10 with a £20 note and tell the shopkeeper to keep the change? No, you would not! Every month you keep your credit card that does not offer 0% interest, you are doing the same thing. Also if you are not regularly checking your monthly expenses and shaving off money to make overpayments on any loans/debts etc. Again you are doing the exact same thing – giving your money away. This is in regards to the unnecessary amounts of interest you pay to the financial institutions each month.
2. Stop spending more than you earn or have. I am sure we have all done this at some point; but it becomes a problem when we make this a lifestyle. This kind of lifestyle will plunge you further and further into debt. The question is, how do you get out of this cycle if you are in it?
    The action needed here is, STOP, THINK, and DON'T ACT! You will need to start constantly checking with yourself if what you are buying is a 'want' or a 'need'.

Many times it is a 'want,' not a 'need' and most 'wants' consist of spending money you probably do not have, which in turn results in debt.

3. Make a change. The fact of the matter is, you will only decide to make a change when you get sick and tired of being sick and tired of your financial situation and feel that you have had enough. It is then and only then that you will be ready to take the first steps to think about attempting to manage your money in a better way.

My objective is to help you develop a mindset that will instantly evoke your thinking. I.e. what you can make happen just by taking the first step. The first step is to get your mind in alignment with your current financial situation. This probably translates into your money, is not working in your best interest at the moment. Once you have accepted this and settled it in your mind, you are good to go because you are thinking smart and ready to work smart.

Now you have some insight into some of the banks' most prominent rules and strategies from the examples and my experiences I have shared. It is time to start making your game plan. From a financial perspective, you will need to start with where you are (in debt or not and with what money you have.) I will share, in chapter three, an example of The Three S's that will begin to shape your mind into becoming a winner in your own financial success game.

TIP

There are many things that will help your credit score.

Make sure you are on the electoral roll, do not miss any payments on your bills (council tax, gas and electric, etc.) close any unused credit/store cards, direct debits and mobile contracts.

Lenders may consider all the credit you have access to like credit cards with credit on them that you are not using, as well as any other debt you owe when making their decisions.

Savings

In todays' society, having some form of savings seem to be a challenge to say the least. For many people, the common complaint is that they are struggling to make ends meet and find it difficult to find something to save.

Nevertheless, regularly going over your monthly outgoings to see what you can cut back on can make a significant difference. You might need to cancel a gym membership you have not used for six months and search comparison sites for the best phone contracts, etc. This may seem like an unnecessary task, but you might pleasantly be surprised by the money you may find that you can either save or utilise.

Savvy savings

Let me share some information about other exciting ways you can save some money.

1. Take a packed lunch to work: The *Guardian* newspaper reported that taking a packed lunch to work can save you over a £1000 a year.

2. Save on your morning coffee: Buying a Starbucks coffee every morning before work will cost you an alarming £554 a year. (Yes shocking I know!) Most supermarkets now do Starbucks and all the different brands of coffees. You could get yours in bulk, take it to work and keep them in your drawer, add your hot water when you get there! No one would ever know, this way you could probably have two cups of Starbucks coffee from the supermarket for the price of one from their shop. What a savvy move!

3. Find deals on holidays: Websites like Travelzoo, Last minute.com and Living Social etc. They have great deals for holidays. One of my daughters discovered that when booking a holiday, prices can go up by as much as £150 just depending on the day and time of day you book. The best times to book are Monday-Wednesday, early in the morning before 12 pm and after 4 pm check it out...

4. Save money when dining out: Websites like Groupon and Living Social have great meal deals. They have offers for places such as The Park Grande in Kensington,

Waldorf Hilton hotel in the Strand, afternoon tea at the Park Lane Hilton in Mayfair, and much more. (No one needs to know you got it on a deal!).

I cannot emphasise enough about signing up to comparison websites. I am signed up to moneysavingexpert.com. I get an email every month with all the good deals and money-saving tips on various products. It's marvelous; anytime I am looking for something like car insurance, travel insurance, and credit cards etc., those sites are my first port of call because they have done most of the groundwork for me. This saves me both time and money!

EXCUSES – I hear people all the time saying things like, "I do not have the time to check through my monthly outgoings". However, research has shown that the average person spends three – five hours a day watching TV, and checking their phone about 150 times. (I am not just referring to young people here!). According to this research, finding the time to go over your outgoings does not appear to be a time problem; but rather a priority problem. If you are serious about having a better quality of life, you will have to change what you are looking at. This is yet another smart move to make if you want a better quality of life!

Regarding being savvy with your outgoings, try doing some of the smart things I discussed. Look at the savings you could make; it is so doable. Again, it is just about making a few changes that will help make a massive financial difference!

Are Your Savings Actually Being Devalued?

For those people who have a disposable income (money left over after all your outgoings have been taken out), I want to give you some insight into what happens with your savings.

Having your money in a bank account is relatively a safe place, but are you experiencing a guaranteed loss? Let us take a look at what happens to your savings after basic **taxes** and **inflation** have had their way!

If you were to deposit £2,000 into a bank account over 12 months that is paying 2% interest, at the end of 12 months, your £2,000 would earn £40.00 in interest. Total amount = £2,040.

You pay 20% tax on £40.00 interest, tax deducted = £8

Your net interest earned after tax is £32.00.

Your net balance after basic tax is deducted would be £2032.00

If inflation is, let's say 2.7% as @ Feb 2018; 2.7% of £2000 equates to £54.00

Your savings amount £2032.00 - original amount plus the inflation increase £2054.00 = £22.00

Your savings have actually been devalued by - £22.00

(As of 6 April 2016 basic rate UK taxpayers pay 20% tax on any personal savings over £1000.)

BE AWARE!

Now I am sure you must be thinking, "Wait a minute, my savings statements never show a loss". This is correct. However, the truth is, your buying power is now reduced. This is a result of a general increase in prices and a fall in the purchasing value of money. What I have just described is *inflation*.

In a nutshell, what you may have been able to buy with

£2,000 the year you deposited it into a savings account would have changed from year to year. Most things, like food, energy and commodities, increase in price every year. So, the fact is, your money will be worth less, but what you are buying will cost you more.

To combat this you will have to earn interest above the rate of inflation, or add to your savings to make up the difference. The example shows the inflation rate of 2.7% (February 2018,) which equated to £54.00 for a savings of £2,000. In theory, £2,000 in 2018 would need to be £2054 in 2019 to have the same value of buying power.

You might want to start thinking about how to make better use of your savings to maximise it. I must highlight that if you have disposable income (money to save), then compound interest is a good thing for savers because it works in your favour. Whatever you have in your savings/investment accounts, interest is added (daily, monthly, quarterly or yearly). Both amounts are added together, i.e. savings plus interest and paid to you hence the term *compounded*. This repetitive cycle is how your money grows.

T Leonard "How are my savings taxed"'. This information is taken from Moneyfact. co.uk 1st May 2018 - (accessed 18 May, 2018)

P Gooding "Consumer price inflation", UK: February 2018. This information is taken from Office for National Statistics 20, March 2018 - (accessed 18 May, 2018)

Now if you are taking out credit, say with a credit/store card, then you will be paying extortionate amounts of interest for this. In the next chapter, you will see the shocking difference between compounded interests for taking out credit compared to compounded interest for savings as shown below.

Example of compounded savings

(Interest rate of 1.3% compounded yearly - added at the end of each year)

Year	Initial deposit	Yearly Deposits	Yearly Interest earned	Total balance
1	£3,000	£1,200.00	£47.43	£4,247.43
2		£1,200.00	£63.65	£5,511.08
3		£1,200.00	£80.08	£6,791.16
4		£1,200.00	£96.72	£8,087.88
5		£1,200.00	£113.58	£9,401.46
Totals	**£3,000**	**£6,000**	**£401.46**	**£9,401.46**

(Figure 4)

This information is taken from Thecalculatorsite.com – (accessed 21 April, 2018.)

The compounded table shows the calculations of a savings account paying a 1.3% interest rate. There is an initial deposit of £3,000, as well as depositing £1,200 for five years = £6,000 Total compounded interest earned for five years = £401.46. In theory, your £9,000 has earned **£401.46** interest in five years.

N.B. As previously mentioned, the buying power for the total amount of £9,401.46 will be worth less than what it is. Inflation rates would have taken place over the five years the money was invested.

There is an old saying that goes, "Those who understand interest earn it, those who don't, pay it".

Let's look at what was covered in this chapter:

1. How to purchase items that you require by using the banks' money at no extra costs
2. When to put your money to better use
3. How to save yourself lots of money by making overpayments on your financial products
4. The importance of treating yourself while you are maximising your money
5. What happens to your savings when it is in the bank

TIP

It is not what you know but what you do with what you know. Action is always required!

Now we have established some of the reasons why you should 'think like a bank', let's explore the psychology of debt, so you can better position yourself for financial success.

CHAPTER 2

The Psychology of Debt

The psychology of debt is quite a broad subject. Many different aspects of it can be somewhat complicated. However, I will be discussing some areas that I feel may be relevant and relatable to you. This information will prove to be beneficial when understanding how you may have arrived at your current financially positon.

My approach is to help you gain insight into how the mind works. This emphasis will highlight how you make your choices and decisions about using your money.

With that being said, we are aware of times in our lives when we may experience unpleasant changes in our circumstances. For example job loss, illness, relationship breakdown or the loss of a loved one etc. Any of these experiences can affect your 'thinking processes'. For example, your perception of the problem can compromise your memory, inhibit your ability to problem solve, think clearly, or stay focused. When your judgement has been impacted in this way, you are more than likely to make unhealthy financial choices.

One of the common reactions to something like this is a lack of self-control in terms of spending. I.e. the pleasurable feelings of 'retail therapy' temporarily soothing the pain. As a result of spending like this, there is the risk of some psychological and financial consequences that can take place if this behavior is not swiftly addressed. For example, experiencing emotional problems, such as depression, anxiety, stress, problematic eating patterns, sleepless nights, disruption to your daily routine and a lack of peace, etc. Not to mention racking up unnecessary debt for purchasing items you cannot afford.

The impact of debt

Being in debt for long periods can cause you to go through a cycle of repetitive emotions from worry to despair. These feelings can leave you feeling emotionally drained and depleted. Worry is inevitable for those who are in this situation however, Bishop TD Jakes once said: "Worry is the interest paid on something that may or may not happen". So, what are the possible outcomes? You either stay in debt for long periods accumulating further debt, or you pay off what you owe.

The reality is worry (or interest, as Bishop Jakes refers to it) will never change or help the situation. It only serves as having a negative impact on your physical and emotional wellbeing. Nevertheless, whatever the reason for being in debt, the solutions are varied and wide-ranging to meet the needs of the individual.

Know that all is not lost. Getting into debt did not happen overnight and getting out of debt is the same. Do not be too hard on yourself; it is a process. Think of it like you are on a journey to a secret destination and along the way you are discovering and learning different things about yourself, such as finding alternative and creative ways to manage and maximise your money. From a psychological perspective, this could be referred to as self-actualisation.

Self-actualisation - refers to a person's desire to discover their talents and strengths, with the intent to maximise their potential. You can relate self-actualisation to money management as follows:

1. Discover your gifts and talents. One idea can make you a millionaire! For example, Colonel Sanders created a fried chicken recipe, and bingo – KFC was founded. The rest is history.
2. Vow to always save money, whether it is £10 a week or £10 a month. It is the principal you are working on, not the amount.
3. Being mindful of your thought processes, i.e. thinking clearly and staying focused. These might seem like simple concepts, but they are powerful mind processes. It is actually a skill to control your thought processes; as a result, the reward will be healthier financial choices.

Here are a few actions you can think about to get you started:

1. Have a budget. I will discuss this further on in the book.

2. Cancel any unnecessary outgoings. Anything you have not used for more than six or eight weeks you are more than likely not going to use. Examples include gym memberships and subscriptions.
3. Find cheaper providers using comparison websites such as moneysupermarket.com for bills and purchases. If you have been with a provider for a year or more, ask if they have any loyalty packages.
4. Once you gain some knowledge and skills on how to manage your money, you can start developing a strategy to maximise it.

Debt from a psychological perspective

From a psychological perspective, the associated areas of the brain that are affected when getting into debt are the prefrontal cortex and the limbic system. Let's refer to the prefrontal cortex as the 'responsible adult'. Some of its functions are to influence and regulate our impulsive decision making, logical reasoning and self-control.

On the other hand, the limbic system can be referred to as the 'mischievous carefree child'. This area of the brain is what makes us want fun and pleasure instantaneously, whatever the cost.

These two parts of the brain are in constant conflict with each other and are battling over which one will take control of what you do every day.

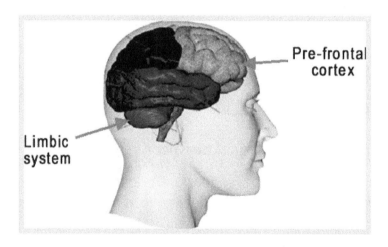

(Figure 5)

An example of the prefrontal cortex winning a battle is having the control over what you spend. I.e., NOT using credit to buy what you cannot afford. A typical senario could be, you're feeling low or upset, buying something to cheer you up, like a new dress or phone can be a great antidote at the time. If you know you do not have the money to do this, and after much deliberation, you decide not to, you have your prefrontal cortex to thank.

An example of the limbic system winning is when that Caribbean cruise which looks so great gets booked up before you can blink. In our current society, no one wants to wait and save anymore. People want things instantly; minimal thought is given about getting burnt by any added costs like extortionate interest rates from borrowing on credit.

If you go ahead and make that purchase, we know what part of the brain won that time and why. Sometimes the prefrontal cortex wins, and other times the limbic system wins. Next time you're thinking of buying something you really cannot afford. Take a few moments to ask yourself which part of your brain seems to be winning the battle. Is it the responsible adult or the mischievous child? In social psychology, this is known as attribution.

Attribution — is the process by which a person explains the causes of behaviour and events.

Hey big spenders!

I once overheard a conversation on a train between three young men in their early twenties. One of them was telling the others how he went out for the night with a friend and spent £3,000 in a nightclub. He went on to say that the friend he was out with said they could pay £50 a month to pay off the credit card. He said he worked out that if they only paid £50 a month towards the debt, it would take them over ten years to pay it off.

Now if that is not 'a moment of pleasure but a lifetime of pain', I don't know what is. That type of spending consists of many contributing factors; i.e., high emotions, entitlement, peer pressure, a lack of self-control and financial knowledge. What happened there was something that would be referred to as *hyperbolic discounting*.

__Hyperbolic discounting__ - is what happens when you discount whatever will happen to you in the future. I.e. consequences (in this case being in debt of £3000 for many years), in exchange for what is happening right now – enjoying the moment. Their poor future will have the burden of being saddled with a back-breaking liability of a credit card debt. This is because they felt they absolutely had to have that night of fun whatever the cost; instead of spending what they could actually afford.

Triggers or significant links

We all have emotional triggers which set off a memory tape in the brain to a past experience, good or bad. The brain forms a connection between a trigger and the feelings with which it is associated. This is known as the *__Availability heuristic__*- A judgment based on the information readily available in memory. Many people are not aware of their triggers or any significant links in connection to their spending habits or debts.

There are various spending patterns that are linked to our triggers. For example, you might find yourself having a hard week at work and need a reward, so you give yourself a treat. Or you have had an argument with your partner which leaves you feeling upset, so you buy yourself something.

Either of these triggers is readily available in our memory to easily recall. As a result, we spend what we do not have, and as a result we convince ourselves that we will pay off the credit or store card as soon as the payment is due. However, this does not always materialise.

These emotional triggers are very common, and if they are something that happens regularly, you can quite easily see how credit can be used to fund this behaviour and accumulate debt.

Discovering what has caused most of your debts, whether it is emotional triggers, an unexpected event or unhealthy decisions will give you a reference point to start from. It is not about blaming yourself or making excuses, but about identifying the areas that would be most helpful for you to begin working on.

How is your relationship with money?

Money is such a complicated matter because it has a significant impact on the way we think, express ourselves and behave appropriately regarding our emotions. Many decisions we make about money are personal to us, and that is reflected in our lives in a personal way.

Most of our views on money have derived from our upbringing, culture, environment, family, friends and financial experiences. Our past involvement with money has a direct impact on our mindset, namely the ability to understand the power of money, i.e. what it can and cannot do.

Whether you believe it or not, we all have a relationship with money, so what is yours? Is it something that is necessary, powerful, beneficial and enjoyable? Alternatively is it a source of misery or a burden? If your relationship with money is positive, it can be used as a tool to enhance the quality of your life. It can help you reach your family's goals, such as building a nice home, having great holidays, and enjoying your desired future.

Whatever you have respect for in life, including money, you will work diligently to maximise its potential. No one buys a stereo with two speakers and only uses one. The same applies to money. If you have £10, then your mindset should be that you want the best out of your £10. This shows that you respect, appreciate and enjoy the pleasure of getting the most out of your money because it has been well spent.

On the other hand, if you do not respect money, you are more than likely to have a negative relationship with it. You will probably see it as something to use frivolously, not really appreciating or respecting it. Therefore, not much thought will be taken when spending it. You can be prone to blowing it without thinking or have little idea of what you have spent it on.

This may be the reason you are accumulating unnecessary amounts of debt. Money is currency, just like the current of the sea, it flows to you or away from you depending on your attitude about it.

Nevertheless, whatever your relationship with money is right now, whether you pay attention to it or not. You can always make changes to improve it.

While I know that money cannot buy happiness, I am sure that many of you will agree that it temporarily helps to soothe our emotions. It can also give us pleasure when things are not going too well. This can be made worse if you are around others who agree with you at the time of your moment of vulnerability.

When we tell ourselves we are entitled to spend what we want, it can be referred to as *'consensual validation'*. This is the mutual affirmation of perspective views of reality. In other words, consensual validation means the agreement or confirmation from yourself and others to spend money because of your current situation/dilemma. This can be perceived as validation to do so – so beware!

As you can see from the various psychological terms I have discussed. A large number of people experience one or more of these terms daily, consciously or subconsciously. This chapter is to help you begin to think more pragmatically about some of your money management practices.

Whether it is the highlighted battles that take place in your brain before you spend or the impact your finances are having on your psychological wellbeing. You are now armed with some information about what is psychologically happening and its influence on your financial decisions.

Throughout this book, you will note how I continuously emphasise that knowledge is power, and the right 'mindset' is key. By the time you have finished this book if the only thing you take away from it is two words - 'knowledge' and 'mindset'. I feel I have accomplished what I set out to do regarding maximising your money. That is to help you 'transform your finances by re-educating your mind'.

Confession time

Having a background in finance and psychotherapy has not exempted me from previously accumulating debt or making a few unhealthy financial choices over the years. Fortunately, I had the knowledge and skills to get myself back on track and reflect on where I possibly went wrong and why. I guess you can call it the perks of the job!

No one is perfect; many successful people have accumulated wealth only to lose it. Sometimes they have regained it and other times they have not. This shows that I am not alone regarding making mistakes, and neither are you. Nelson Mandela rightly said, "I never lose, I either win or learn."

When I hear people say they are in debt or are struggling with their finances, my first thoughts are how I can help them. I feel certain that I can help them change one small thing that could possibly make a big difference. Of course, this is what I do!

Every day I pray that I can make a difference in the life of someone I meet. Being a Psychotherapist, this is practically inevitable and that is why I am so passionate about what I do. However, equally outside of my consulting room, I experience this opportunity almost every time with the people I meet. The candid humour that I have adopted from my mother seems to serve me well in achieving this.

Why not take a look at what you have just learnt. Do take a few minutes to ask yourself the following questions:

1. Can you identify what has been influencing your spending patterns?
2. Can you see how you may have accumulated your debt?
3. Can you identify any of your triggers and if you can, what are they?
4. Can you identify your relationship with money?
5. What have you learnt from this chapter?

TIP

Seek help, i.e. some form of intervention when you find your normal daily routine being compromised because of money challenges. The support you seek can be anything from debt advice and support (practical help), counselling (therapy), or a visit to your GP (medical assistance).

Now you have an insight into the psychology of debt, we will go on to the next chapter that has some nuggets you can apply this knowledge to.

CHAPTER 3

5 Golden Financial Educational Nuggets

This chapter intends to share with you five financial golden nuggets that will leave you with a wealth of knowledge. It will also position you to make better informed financial decisions. Bishop Jakes once said, "If bad decisions got you in, then good decisions will get you out".

By the end of this chapter, these nuggets will now be yours. You can either invest them to maximise their value, by applying them to the financial areas of your life that have been challenging. Alternatively, you can leave them in this book and not change a thing. Your nuggets, your choice!

The areas I will be covering are as follows:

1. Raising your awareness of the different types of debt
2. Why it is essential to shop around for the right financial products
3. 'Think like a bank' regarding mortgage payments
4. Speed up your debt repayments
5. Five ways to beat the banks' at their own game

Golden Nugget #1

The different types of debt

Many people in society have no idea that there are different types of debt the banks' systems use. The need to borrow money seems to be far more pressing than finding out the smartest way to do this. It is imperative to arm yourself with the right information.

Research and educate yourself to fully understand how financial products work, and most importantly explore the long and short-term financial impact. Taking these points into account will prevent you from accumulating unnecessary debt and negatively affecting your quality of life.

There are **three** fundamental kinds of debt which we will now look at:

1. Revolving debt

This type of debt is associated with credit and store cards. With these products, each month the debt goes on and on until you ultimately pay it off. There is no set end date. This is what I would call the 'treadmill effect'. You may be putting a lot of effort into making minimal payments, but the debt does not decrease. In fact, the debt appears to increase due to the interest being added to your outstanding balance daily. (To add salt to the wound, financial institutions normally charge additional fees, and this varies between lenders).

What I have just described is *compounded interest*. Compound interest is interest calculated on the amount you use. For example, if you were to take out a credit card with a £10,000 limit which **does** not have **0%** interest, once you have used whatever amount, be it £10.00 or £10,000 that money starts to accumulate interest daily.

If you are only paying the minimum amount on the outstanding balance, your minimum payments have no real effect on reducing the debt. In fact, it may just cover last month's interest that you have been charged. The only positive effect minimum payments have is that they show you are paying your credit card each month as agreed by your bank. This is good for your credit score/report (as previously discussed).

Each month **new** interest charges are **added** to last month's balance, in addition to any further money spent. Hence the term *compound*, both the new interest and the outstanding amount are being compounded together monthly repeatedly increasing the debt.

Example

On an outstanding credit card balance of £10,000 with an 18.9% APR, making the minimum payment of 1% of the balance plus interest or £5, whichever is the greatest can cost you £14,342 in interest.

Can you see how easily banks' are making vast amounts of money from us? A £10,000 debt on a credit card could turn into a £24,342 and can take around 37 years and five months to pay off. The bank can make about £14,342 profit just by compounding monthly interest to the initial £10,000 used. We are like lambs to the slaughter; there is no escape. The difference between the interests on your deposited savings (DS) and borrowing credit is extortionate. For banks' it is a win/win situation.

For the borrower, we lose every time because we end up paying back more than what we originally intended. Whatever money we save, if we were to borrow that same amount back from the bank, we would always pay back inflated amounts. That is why banks' are successful and remain successful. They are indeed experts at their game.

2. Fixed debt

Fixed debt is a loan for a set period, i.e., 25 years to pay off a mortgage etc. Although debt is not a good thing to have in general, some debts are unavoidable, such as having a mortgage. What I am saying is, if there is any such thing as a good debt this type of debt works best because the total amount you will pay is given upfront.

With this type of debt, all interest and finance charges are included and agreed at the initial signing of the contract. Your monthly payments are made up of paying part of your payment to the principal amount (that is, the amount borrowed) and part to the accumulated daily interest. By consistently paying the agreed monthly amount, you will see your debt decreasing until it is paid off at the end of the fixed period. This is the opposite of revolving debt.

EXAMPLE

Revolving debt
VS
Fixed debt

Take a look at how a revolving debt VS a fixed debt for the same amount can have a detrimental impact on your finances.

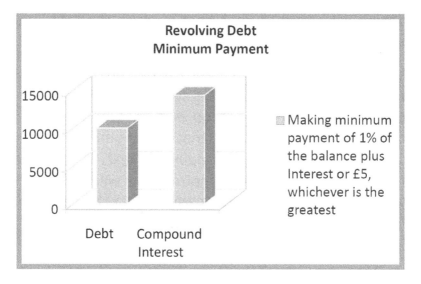

(Figure 6)

£10,000 @ 18.9% could take up to 37 years and 5 months to pay off

Revolving debt interest paid: £14,342

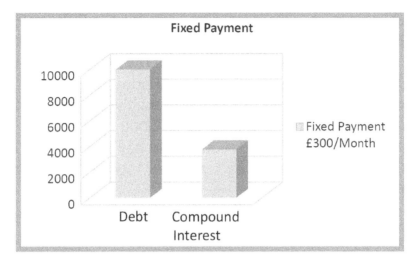

(Figure 7)

£10,000 @ 18.9% could take up to *3 years and 10 months to pay off*

Fixed debt interest paid: £3,770

N.B. *the figures quoted are only estimates of the costs and time to repay.*

This Information is taken from Moneysavingexpert.com – "credit card calculator" – (accessed 9 July, 2018.)

As you can see, the examples highlight the difference between the interest you could be paying and the time it can take to pay off the debt. Regarding the revolving debt by making the minimum payment, you could potentially pay around £14,342 in interest, and it can take roughly 37 years and five months to pay off. For the same £10,000 debt with a fixed monthly payment of £300, you would pay around £3,770 in interest and take three years and ten months to pay it off. What a difference!

Something you must be aware of, if you decide to fix your monthly payment, you will need to ensure that it is more than the initial minimum payment set by the bank. First check your bank statement, which will show the minimum amount payable. Then increase your payment to a fixed amount even if it is only minimal.

For example, if the banks' minimum payment for your debt is £15.50, you need to increase your fixed payment above that, say to £25.00.

The key in this part of the game is to make the smart move of increasing your payments to be more than the banks' initial minimum payment for your debt. If you do not check this information out before fixing your monthly payments, you could find your debt revolving for years and years as opposed to paying it off in a fraction of the time (as shown in the example).

All it takes is for you to know how to play the banks' game, and you will always win and be quid's in!

TIP

In essence, it is not what you borrow that is the problem, it is *how* you borrow. If you need to borrow large amounts of money, aim for a fixed loan as opposed to a revolving credit card. At least you will know up front how much your total payment will be. Use the comparison websites for the best interest rates. Their calculators will give you a good indication of your monthly repayments and the time it will take to pay off the amount you have borrowed.

3. Interest only

Interest-only products, such as an interest-only mortgage and interest on overdrafts, are by far the most difficult to understand and give the financial institutions great joy. For example, say you borrow £50,000 at the start of a loan for 15 years. With an interest-only product, you are only paying the daily interest charged on the £50,000; you are not touching the £50,000 debt at all. At the end of the 15-year term, you would have paid the bank all the interest due but will still owe them the whole amount of £50,000 you initially borrowed.

N.B. Before you decide to take out an interest-only product, you must set up a savings plan or an investment to save for the entire principal (in this case the principal is £50,000). If this is not in place at the end of the term, you will have to cough up this money from somewhere. For example, remortgage your property or make alternative arrangements with your financial provider to start paying off the principal.

Again can you see how this is another one of the banks' main winning strategies? This is all done with our deposited savings/investments, which they loan out to others while they coin in all that interest.

TIP

From today, financial institutions do not have to be the only ones that are successful with our money. We can also be successful with our own money, so continue to read on to find out how.

Golden Nugget #2

Shop for the Right Financial Products

I cannot stress enough how important it is to have the right financial products to make your money work for you. For example, 0% credit cards if (possible) and best interest rate loans, etc. Again, check the comparison websites that I have mentioned throughout this book. They are great for finding the best top ten financial products for your needs.

It is also good to talk to other people. I had a life insurance cover for £100,000, with monthly premiums of £27.16. Then I spoke to a friend who told me about her life insurance with a company called Vitality. They are a great company, and they offer many benefits, such as discounts to Champneys health spa. (That is right up my street) up to 50% of gym membership fees, discount on Cineworld and Vue cinema tickets, etc. Definitely look it up!.

Well, I made some enquiries, and as a result, I ended up with an increased life cover of £130,000. In summary, I got £30,000 more cover than I originally had, with an approximately £10 lower premium a month. Please note, life cover is dependent on several things including age and health etc.

The key here is; not to become complacent with the financial products you already have. You can shop around each year, or when a product comes to an end. This would mean you are following the rules in your game plan.

Banks' are continually changing their financial products to keep up with the demands of their customers and trends of the financial markets to stay on top. You will also be doing the same by shopping around for the best financial products to stay on top of your finances. The great thing is, there is so much competition out there between financial institutions; that you are more than likely to get a good deal.

It may take a little time to get all your financial products in order, but once they are in place, you are good to go. Let's give the banks' a run for their money; by doing what they do best. Which is making **our** money work for us instead of working for them. To win in the game, you have to be in it so get on board!

Where you are, today financially did not happen overnight. If it is helpful to you, retrace some of your steps to see where you may have made some mistakes to avoid further pitfalls. Then, armed with your new-found knowledge, you can start making smart choices.

TIP

Having the right mindset coupled with the right knowledge, you are guaranteed to win!

Golden Nugget #3

Think Like a Bank when Making Mortgage Payments

Most people long to see the day when they will become mortgage free. Well, there is a clever way you can make that happen sooner rather than later without having to add a penny to your monthly repayments. Some people may already know this, but for those who do not, you soon will. I am sure you may be thinking, "I need this information now!" So here it is.

All you have to do is pay your mortgage fortnightly (every two weeks) as opposed to monthly and you will be saving thousands. Let me show you how to do this step by step for ease:

1. There are 52 weeks in a calendar year.
2. There are 48 weeks or (12 monthly payments) in a mortgage banking year.
3. The difference between a calendar year and a mortgage banking year is four weeks, which equates to one month.
4. Paying your mortgage twice a month, you will regain

those extra four weeks.

5. Banks' have set up 12 monthly mortgage payments even though there are 52 weeks in a year, which equates to 13 months: 52÷4=13.

6. Some months have five weeks; however, banks have cleverly worked in the outstanding four weeks over a 12-month period.

7. Making 26 fortnightly payments enables you to successfully pay one extra month per year on your mortgage, saving you thousands of pounds in interest and reducing your term.

Example

Monthly payment table

Monthly payments per year	Amount paid per month	Total calculations per year
12	£1,000 per month	£1,000 × 12 months = £12,000

(Figure 8)

Fortnightly payment table

Fortnightly payments per year	Amount paid fortnightly	Total calculations per year	Fortnightly mortgage savings for the year
26	£500 every two weeks	£500 x 26 weeks = £13,000	£1,000

(Figure 9)

As you can see from the tables, by paying your mortgage fortnightly, your repayment mortgage savings for the year would be £1,000.

The steps that need to be taken to put this into action are as follows:

1. Contact your bank to tell them you would like to start paying your mortgage fortnightly. If they ask why tell them you have seen the light!!
2. If they say it is ok to do this, then you need to ask the bank if the extra two fortnightly payments you accumu-

lated that equates to one month will be applied solely to your principal (the amount you initially borrowed for your mortgage) and not used as a regular mortgage payment. If these two payments are applied to the principal, that is what saves you thousands and reduces the number of years left on your mortgage. Be sure to cancel your monthly direct debit.

3   The next thing to do is set up two standing orders, one on the date that your mortgage is normally due and one for 14 days before that for this to work correctly.
For example, if your mortgage is due on the 15th of the month, set up one standing order for half of the monthly amount - using this example it would be £500.00 for the 1st of the month and the other £500.00 for the 15th. **Both** payments must be made each month by the original mortgage due date (i.e.,15th).

4. They may well say that this is not possible, because they will not be getting all the interest they were banking on to make their profit. Nevertheless, still go ahead and set up your two standing orders to make your fortnightly payments.

They cannot tell you how to pay your mortgage. As we all know, the emphasis banks' and financial institutions make is to ensure you pay your full repayments each month. As long as they get their money, it should not be a problem.

What do you think would happen to your mortgage if you were to increase your mortgage payments each month (by any amount) and pay that fortnightly? I tell you what will happen; you will be saving substantial amounts of money if you combine both of these strategies.

TIP

It is time to take that step; before long you will have mastered the fortnightly repayment method and made another big win in this financial game!

Golden Nugget #4

Speed up Your Debt Repayments

Most people have debts they are paying off without any thought or strategy. There is a saying that goes "if you fail to plan, you plan to fail". Again, the three rules of the game (Structure + Strategy = Success) need to be applied to win the debt battle.

EXAMPLE

Debts	Interest rate	Repayment	Term
£2,000	21.9%	£60.00	4 yrs 2 months
£3,500	19.9%	£100.00	4 yrs 3 months
£3,000	17.9%	£71.50	5 yrs 4 months

(Figure 10)

STRUCTURE – Identified financially challenged area - credit card debt

The structure here is to eradicate the debt that is charging the highest rate of interest. Once that has been eradicated, move on to the next one until you have worked your way through them all. I have used a combination of three accumulated debts with monthly repayments consisting of £60, £100 and £71.50, totalling £231.50)

This information is taken from Moneysavingexpert.com - "credit card calculator" - (accessed 21 April, 2018.)

STRATEGY - Plan your action - Take the following steps

In this case, the debt for £2,000 is charging the highest rate of interest 21.9% APR. The first step is to reduce the other two debts' repayments to the minimum, which could be £35 (instead of £71.50) and £40 (instead of £100). Each month, add the money you have kept back from the other two debts to the debt with the highest rate of interest until it is cleared. Once cleared, you have now freed up money to work on the next debt and so forth.

SUCCESS – You are in control of your money - debt-free

To recapitulate: You started out with paying £231.50 for three debts. You minimised the repayments on the two debts with lower interest rates and took that money to increase the repayments on the debt with the most expensive interest rate.

When the first debt is paid off, you can now use the same amount you started with £231.50 to pay off the two outstanding debts, and so on. Eventually, you would have paid off all three debts and freed up £231.50. Apply this same strategy while you are working through all your other debts.

Now you can begin to make some smart choices with your money. For example, you can start paying some of your bills such as insurances, TV license, and memberships annually as it works out cheaper. You will now free up the money you would have been paying out for some of those monthly bills. This is how you will start to accumulate disposable income (income available after all your expenses have been paid).

TIP

Use this concept whenever you have multiple debts. It works every time, it's smart, and it proves that you are becoming becoming financially smart too. Make it fun and enjoyable, that way it will be more sustainable.

Golden Nugget #5

Five Ways to Beat the Banks at Their Own Game

1. Change Your Bank Account

Many banks' are now very competitive; they have various offers to attract you to transfer your accounts over to them. These offers can be anything from initial cash incentives to percentage cashback on purchases and travel insurances etc. (Please read the small print, as some of these incentives are for limited periods). Statistics show that most people stay with their banks' for about 17 years, so do shop around for one that might be more beneficial to you.

2. Be a Smart Credit Card Holder

Choose a card with a good reward scheme, for example – the American Express Platinum Card will give you 5% cash back for the first three months (*max £2,000 of spending, so max cash back £100*), then tied ongoing cashback. Be aware, the offers on cards are subject to change, so please read all the small print before applying for any credit card.

3. Don't Make Financial Experts Fat on Commission

Many times, your bank will try to sell you some of their internal products. Look at whether they are suitable for you before you take them out. You need to check what you are paying for.

Historically, many people simply did not realise that they were sold Payment Protect Insurance (hence the mis-sold PPI fiasco). My suggestion would be research and research again. Do your homework before signing up for any financial product. Your goal should be to invest in something that will maximise your money not decrease it.

4. Don't Go Straight to Your Bank for Financial Products

Some financial products are often overpriced, meaning they have higher interest rates. An independent financial advisor or mortgage broker will search the whole financial market to get you the best deals. As opposed to most banks' using the products they have in-house.

The same goes for credit cards, as I mentioned previously. Websites such as moneysupermarket.com can steer you in the right direction and supply you with lots of sound information about the best financial products.

5. *Once You're Out of Debt, STAY Out of Debt*

Debt funds the banks' success. In chapter three of this book, I explained the Three S's – Structure + Strategy = Success. Hopefully, by now, you will have some idea of how to factor the Three S's into your game plan. You will be using some of the banks' own rules so you can succeed while using their money.

NOW is the time to turn things on their head and apply these same rules to yourself. Once you begin to see results, there will be no turning back. Wow! You can begin the journey leading to the destination called 'financial independence'.

Think about how that could feel? What would it look like?

Now test yourself on the following questions:

1. How many different types of debts are there?
2. What is the difference between compounded interest for savings and borrowing?
3. What should you do before taking out any financial products?

4. How many weeks are there in a banking mortgage year?
5. What is the one thing you will take away from this chapter?

TIP

Who would not want a golden nugget? The value of one can change your life forever. I have given you five! After reading, digesting and implementing some or all of these nuggets into your financial matters, your life should never remain the same. The choice is yours. Pastor Matthew Ashimolowo once said. "No one else has an investment in your personal life as you do".

CHAPTER 4

Facing Money Problems

Many people experiencing money problems want to know how they can change their financial situation for the better. This is possible, and you can make it happen even though you may be surprised by some of the information I am about to share.

According to the Financial Conduct Authority (FCA), half of the UK population is financially vulnerable, (as discussed in chapter one).

Have you ever stopped to think about how financially vulnerable you might be?

Take a few moments to consider these questions:

1. What would happen if you lost your job?
2. What if you became ill and could not work?
3. What if your relationship broke down?
4. Do you have any financial plans in place for a rainy day or the future?

The financial impact of any of these situations could be very damaging. I know these thoughts may seem daunting, but at some point, they will need your consideration. I can see some people thinking, "Well, all I need to do is win the lottery, and I will be sorted." On one hand that may be true, but how likely is that to happen in reality? I will leave these thoughts with you.

You can take control of your finances and turn them around with my support. I have been through financial challenges myself and have over 20 years of banking experience. Therefore, I feel qualified to help you.

My money challenge, my money solution

Let me tell you about a financial difficulty I experienced and how I dealt with it.

Back in 1993 I was in my 30's, I became a single mother with three young children aged six years and under. I had a mortgage, a part-time job, and a car to run, so I had to be very resourceful with my money, meaning every penny counted. My brain felt like it was calculating morning, noon and night. Daily, I worked out everything I needed to spend, from school dinner money to mortgage payments. I used to keep a note pad close by with a breakdown of my daily outgoings, which I regularly checked to make sure I was able to meet our needs.

Shopping was the most challenging. I shopped in about four supermarkets each week to get the best bargains; that was until someone introduced me to a supermarket called Lidl's. This is when my life changed! I got such good value for my money, and the best part of this was I could practically do all my shopping in one shop. The marvellous thing for my children and me was, we were now eating like kings and queens!

However, I desperately knew that at some point, something would have to change. Calculating every penny each day was a challenge and very draining. I needed a better quality of life, and I knew that only I could make that happen.

Now and then, my financial situation made me feel overwhelmed and anxious. What kept me going was my memories of watching my mother juggle her money amazingly. I used to think back to those days and concluded that it most definitely had to be a skill that she possessed, as we lacked nothing, and it felt like we had everything.

I remember on the odd occasion when we ran out of squash; my mother would make us a delicious, refreshing jug of sugar and water with slices of lemon and ice (an old Jamaican beverage). I feel it is essential for me to remember those days. I am very mindful about my humble beginnings because it is the anchor that keeps me grounded. Things have changed since then; I don't think I would have gotten away with giving my children the 'sugar and water' beverage in this day and age!

Isn't it incredible how history has a way of repeating itself to some degree? Even though I often struggled financially, the people around me were amazed at what I could do with the minimal money I had. This was because I juggled my money to maximise every penny.

Someone once said to me that I must have a sugar daddy. To their surprise, I said, "Yes, I do, His name is Jesus, and He definitely supplies all my needs! Someone else remarked that they had never met anyone who could go to a market and get three outfits for her kids with £10. Little did they know my mother, who had six children would have bought £10 worth of material and made six outfits for us - by hand, at that!

Another person told me that I have 'champagne taste with Coca-Cola money'. Well, I feel safe enough to say that I have moved up in life since then, whereby I still have champagne taste but with Prosecco money.

Ultimately, the solution to your money challenges is your mindset towards money. I have just shared with you that regardless of how much or how little money you have, knowing how to manage it will help you get the best out of it.

I am sure my situation at the time as a single mother, etc., would have been a lot different if I had the wrong mindset and attitude. (I.e. the belief that my family would not be able to survive on my minimal budget). I could have been left feeling defeated and hopeless about being incapable of providing for our basic needs.

Other contributing factors that affect your finances

Research shows nearly one in three 'Relate' clients (a counselling service for couples) say that debt has contributed to the breakdown of their relationship. One in five clients says debt has a considerable impact on their relationships with their children. So, as you can see, debt is a problem that cannot be ignored.

The Financial Conduct Agency and comparethemarket.com did further research. As of December 2017, they found that more than 6 million people in the UK do not believe they will ever be debt-free. 4.1 million people are already in severe financial difficulty. It also found that people between the ages of 25 and 34 accumulate the most debt. The average person in the UK has a debt of £8,000 – not including their mortgage repayments. Also, 62% of the population said they were often worried about their levels of personal debt.

From the statistics above, you can see that money management challenges have no regard for age or gender. From childhood to adulthood, you are more than likely to live in a household affected by some form of debt.

AD Bradley, 'An investigation into debt and relationships "In Too Deep". This information is taken from Relate, 23 Nov 2017, (accessed 16 Dec, 2017).

M Brignal, 'Borrowing and Debt' Average UK Debt at £8,000 Per Person (not including the mortgage), This information is taken from, The Guardian, 30 Oct 2017, (accessed 16 Dec, 2017).

Chapter 5

Never Too Young to Start

In this chapter, I would like to convey the importance of believing that it is never too early to start managing and maximising money. I aim to encourage families to work together to help their children/grandchildren develop appropriate money management skills and techniques. Hopefully, this knowledge will equip them to appreciate and understand the value of money to make informed decisions.

I am passionately interested in the financial education of young people because financial management is an essential part of their social development. The objective is to build their confidence, so they can actively participate in the future growth of the economy.

For most of society, the subject of money is first taught at home. If you grew up in a household where you were encouraged to think about money, whether positively or negatively, this would have primarily influenced your attitude and behaviour toward it.

For example, if your household has a positive outlook on money, whereby thoughts and questions are shared. I.e., "Can we afford this?" or "Do we need it?" This type of questioning would begin to evoke young peoples' thought processes and help them exercise their thinking. It can also assist them when making decisions for other situations.

On the other hand, if there is a lack of money, or poor money management, such as continually using credit to make purchases for themselves or the household. Chances are young peoples' money management choices, and decisions may well be poor, regardless of their economic status or financial situation in the future.

This becomes more evident if the young person goes into a profession that earns them an excellent salary. The limbic system part of the brain (mischievous carefree child) will tend to dominate and influence their decisions. They may not have much regard for their money and also find it difficult to manage. It is clearly not about the money but rather their knowledge, experiences, attitude and mindset about it.

Where it all began for me

Thankfully from a young age, I observed how both of my parents managed their money. They did this in very different ways, and I gleaned the tools I believed I could use from them both. My mother had six children and had to work to a tight budget to make every penny count.

She would take whatever money she had (which wasn't much) and make something great out of it. Whether her money was for food or clothes for the family, she had an amazing ability to stretch it with apparent ease (although I am sure this was not the case). The one thing I will never forget is that we never went without anything. So, in my mind, I thought if my mother could do such a great job with six children, I should have no problem with half that amount.

On the other hand, my dad was quite frugal; he made sure he maximised every penny. Back in the 60's, he had a property portfolio which consisted of four properties: two houses, and a dry cleaner in Jamaica and a house in England. Looking back, I think I can proudly say with confidence that he was an undercover entrepreneur!

I adopted some of their mindsets, and that is what has kept me driven and focused on maximising my finances.

I implemented a large part of the knowledge and experiences I gained from both my parents, into raising my children, making the necessary adaptions. From a very young age, their reward for doing their chores was either pocket money to buy treats or save their money, and that would go towards paying for their holiday.

As young as they were, I was getting them to think about making wise choices and important decisions that would affect their quality of life. Each year they made the right choice! It did not take them long to make a decision or give it much thought because they loved going on holiday.

Although I was a single parent at the time, we had a holiday abroad every year. When we travelled, each one of my children would have their rucksacks full to the brim. I bet you are thinking, "With what?" Yes, you guessed right. It was not dolls or electronic games; it was pasta, rice, biscuits, gravy and tea bags etc. That is what I call being resourceful! Most of the time, all I would have to buy was meat and vegetables when we got to our holiday destination.

Taking most of our shopping in our luggage might seem unconventional, but it meant that we had more money to spend on our holiday. Sometimes my children complained about carrying the load in their rucksacks; I had to explain to them each year that this is what we needed to do to have more spending money. I also had to highlight that they were going on holiday every year, and not everyone was privileged to have that opportunity or luxury.

What was I teaching them? I was teaching them the value of money and the importance of working for whatever they want or need in life.

My children have adopted many of my money management practices and skills. Such as, they are focusing on saving for a deposit for their own home, not having any debt, using credit in the right way, as explained in the previous chapters. These practices are helping to build up their credit score so they can purchase a property when they are ready to do so.

They seem to be doing a great job, so I am pleased to say I must have done a relatively good job with them to experience these outcomes.

Daddy's pep talk

I remember my dad having one of his pep talks with me when I was in my teens. He had his way of trying to get things across to me when he wanted to impart some form of wisdom. He would often start by saying. "You do not have to take my foolish advice". In other words, what he really meant was, you need to listen to my good piece of advice.

He started off by saying, "Never, ever rent a property. Every property I have had, I have always bought." He went on to say that I should always own my own home. He said with renting you could pay your rent for 25 years and the week you miss a payment, even though you have been paying it for so many years, you could lose your home. You would have nothing to show for all the rent you paid over the years. At that point, in my mind, a seed was sown. I knew I didn't want that to happen to me. As a result, a few years later, in the 80's, at the age of 21, I bought my first property.

Reflecting on this, I think that the reason I felt confident enough to step out and purchase my first property at a relatively young age was that I saw the evidence of what my dad did. Back in Jamaica while living with his grandmother, he saved as much as he could out of his wages until he had a deposit to buy his first house. He then rented that house out and used some of the rent coupled with his wages to buy his second home and subsequent properties.

My dad used this strategy for creating his property portfolio. Every year he would tell my siblings and me the same story about how he got his properties. He really wanted to make sure we all got the message. I can now confirm that his storytelling worked well because we all own our homes, and a couple of us have more than one. What he said carried weight, but what he actually did carried more weight. A well-known statement is said that "We are the product of our environment".

Ask yourself, what environment(s) are you currently in or have you been exposed to? Your answer should give you an indication of where you are in life today. You see, we are only as strong as our minds; our minds strengthen our belief system. If you believe you can do something, you will; if you believe you can't, you won't. Your mind is where success or failure is initially established.

Thank you, dad!

Property Cohort (a property information hub) state that a study revealed, the average adult will spend more than £63,000 on rent before they buy their first home.

People who have made it onto the property ladder in the last five years paid an average £625 a month in rent before they were able to buy.

The study also revealed that on average, renters will be lining landlords' pockets for eight-and-a-half years before getting a place of their own.

Looking at these statics, I know my dad was completely right!

This Information is taken from Property Cohort – (accessed 12 Dec, 2018)

In todays society, many children compare what they have i.e. the latest trainers to what other children have, either at school or in their environment. Peer pressure is definitely on the increase and has become very problematic. Working in a primary school as a Therapist, part of the issues children face such as depression, anxiety and stress etc is due to some form of pressure. Not having the latest game or trainers, falls into this category. Can you see how important it is to introduce them to the relevance and value of money from as early as possible?

Set a Good Example

Setting a good example is paramount. As mentioned earlier most childrens' money management practices develop from what they have been exposed to. Such as seeing their parents budgeting, saving and using things like credit cards and loans to purchase items.

When it comes to learning about saving and money management skills, using visuals, making it fun and being interactive can work very well. You can be creative about what you think would work best for you and your children. Saving apps are great; there is a fantastic one for kids called 'Go Henry'. This app will probably do most of the work for you in terms of teaching them to budget and save. Check it out in the appendix.

A few more ideas are money-saving charts, using different envelopes and jars for different savings, and rewards for saving money. Playing games like Monopoly and Rich Dad Cashflow for Kids is another good option focused on money management and the importance of planning for the future.

As I said earlier in this chapter, I gleaned my money management skills from both my parents and developed them to make them what they are today. We all know that most young children aspire to be like their parents in one way or another. This compelling fact helps with this process because they are more inclined to engage in what you are teaching them.

Now, I know some people may not have been able to glean financial knowledge from their parents. Nonetheless, the real message is, 'You are never too young or too old to start'. Try starting from where you are today.

Talk About Money

A large number of parents have the view that they do not want to worry or bother their children about financial challenges. On one hand, that may be good, but unfortunately, we live in a society where many people have an entitlement mentality. This entitlement mentality has filtered down to as young as primary school children.

Highlighting the fact that your family is financially challenged at a particular time is a discussion that can help a family come together. It can act as a place to start thinking about different ways to work through a situation. For example, the household could do an individual budget, whereby the youngest to the eldest (if possible) list their income and outgoings.

Doing a family budget will allow the children to see what funds are available or unavailable. If they are asking for something which the family budget clearly shows there is no money to pay for it, then you can encourage them to start thinking about some alternative decisions they may need to make.

Having discussions about various family needs is another way to involve everyone. Ideas and suggestions on how different financial obligations could be met can be a fun and provocative exercise. It can begin to help everyone think about what they may be able to do, such as cut back on certain things to assist in meeting a family need.

Suggesting children try saving for what they want or wait until there is money to pay for it. What do you think they can learn from this? The answer is, they will start to understand the difference between wants and needs. For example, they should start learning to ask themselves whether they really need, or simply want a particular item. Once this begins to happen, they are on their way to making smart decisions about their money.

Now you have read this chapter, try answering the following questions:

1. Where did you learn your money management practices?
2. What is your household outlook on money; is it positive or negative?
3. What are your thoughts about doing an individual family budget?
4. Do your children know the difference between wants and needs?
5. Do you think you are setting a good example?

TIP

Whether you are a parent, grandparent, aunt, or uncle etc. I urge you to engage in some form of play with your children to start them thinking about creative ways they can be savvy with their money.

Nowadays, some children have more money in their possession than adults – which they do not like letting go of at times, I must add. Use any of the suggestions I have shared or create some of your own that might be more appropriate for your family.

Chapter 6

Budgeting the Smart Way

In this chapter, I am going to cover the following:

1. The purpose of budgeting
2. How to budget
3. Why you should budget
4. Budgeting the smart way

At the end of this chapter, you should have gained some insight into the key points of budgeting and how to budget the smart way.

rpose of Budgeting

budgeting may seem like an old fashioned thing to do, ally to some young people. However, I am here to tell you ..at if you do not keep track of your income and expenditure, you will end up going completely off track financially.

Starting somewhere is essential. I believe that budgets are important irrespective of how little or how much money you have. I cannot emphasise this enough. Not monitoring your finances is one of the key factors that cause debt.

Setting a budget allows you to take the first steps in getting your finances in order. Another significant rule in this 'game plan' is about taking control of what money you have. Having control will always give you the right amount of buying power. Once you are armed with this buying power, you are in a position to make informed decisions about what you can spend.

How to Budget

When creating your budget, you can start by using your last three months' bank and credit card statements to give you an idea of all your monthly income and expenditure. The next step is to undertake the following:

1. List all your income and expenditure.
2. Set a realistic budget.
3. Ensure that you list absolutely everything. Small expenses such as regular trips to a fast-food restaurant or morning cups of coffee from the corner shop can add up to alarming amounts (as you have been shown). Everything must be included, or more to the point, taken out if you want to save money!
4. Deduct all your expenditures from your income to see what is left.
5. Whatever is left that is what you have to live on.
6. If there is nothing left, and you do not have enough for your expenses, this is where your work begins.
7. Start checking each item on your expenditure list to see what is absolutely necessary.
8. Check to see if you can get any better deal elsewhere. Look for cheaper phone contracts, broadband, and car insurance. Your best bet is to check this all out in one place, like the comparison websites. You are going to have to do

the work if you want to maximise your money. It will really be worth it in the long run.

9. You will have to be consistent for this to work properly. Eventually, you should get into a flow of doing this every month. Hopefully, by doing so, you will start seeing a pattern of your money beginning to get into some order.

10. Make a record of your budget somewhere that is easily accessible.

There is no excuse anymore. Online are some fantastic free apps to help you do this (they are listed in the appendix at the back of the book). The apps do everything from tracking your finances and seeing what areas you are spending in, to connecting your bank accounts, viewing what's coming in, and setting spending goals.

Example

(Figure 11)

If you don't want to use an app, then you can get a budget calculator online again from a site like 'moneysavingsexpert. com' to use on your phone or tablet, etc. These apps or budget calculators can calculate everything each time you spend, as well as give you your new balance, so you know exactly what you have left in your accounts.

If you really don't want to use a computer, then it is simple; it's back to the old basic pen and paper and a calculator. What I am emphasising here is, you really need to find something that works for you and use it.

Example

Single person's Income and Expenditure budget

*Income	£1,783
Less: Expenditure	
Rent/Mortgage	£600
Shopping	£180
Utilities/Phones	£120
Cards & Loans	£50
Pension	£35
Travel	£35
Savings	£50
Car expenses	£150
Personal care	£50
Entertainment	£150
Miscellaneous	£100
Total Expenditure	£1,520
Balance	£263

(Figure 12)

According to the *incometaxcalculator.org.uk,* the, average gross annual earnings for full-time employees in 2017 was £26,500. After-tax and national insurance is deducted your net take-home is £1,783 per month.

Whatever your income, the concept of budgeting is the same. It is basically just keeping a detailed track of all your income and expenditure.

Why Should You Budget?

Surprisingly enough, regardless of what you do for a living whether you are an Investment Banker or a Baker - the issues with finances seem to remain the same. For many people, whatever way they try to manage it, more often than not, it is still a struggle to make ends meet.

In fact, a large percentage of people marginally live above their breadline. Most of the time, people give up hope of trying to figure this frustrating situation out, which in turn leaves them feeling somewhat helpless. Simply budgeting could be your solution to this problem.

In the previous chapter, I discussed various ways of engaging everyone in money management practices, whether you are a child, parent, single or married. Whatever your status, budgeting applies to us all.

Once you have set up a budget and it is functional, tracking what is coming in and going out will be simple. Use any of the budgeting tools I have mentioned as this will help you begin to see a clear picture of your spending patterns. When this happens, you can start to alter and prioritise what you do with your money to help you stay within your means. Applying this knowledge will indicate that half of the battle is won.

However, knowing what to do is one thing, but sticking to it is entirely another. Again using the budgeting tools mentioned is excellent for this. Some of the tools will accurately track your transactions and constantly highlight when/if you are in the red. Seeing your balance in the red for long periods should start to encourage you to change some of your spending habits to get yourself back in the black.

The saying that goes, "out of sight, out of mind" is so true. Not budgeting means you will have no idea of what your finances are up to, which makes it all too easy to keep spending. Now that you are tracking what you spend, it will begin to make you consciously think before you feel like spending frivolously.

Budgeting the Smart Way

Once you get used to having a budget; I would recommend you use as many budgeting tools to assist in maintaining a successful budget.

Being resourceful; i.e. having a budget is one of the best ways to make your money work for you. Let's recap on some of the things that have been discussed in this book to make that happen:

1. Shop around when doing your shopping in-store or online, look for better deals.
2. Track everything you spend.
3. Review your spending habits regularly.
4. If possible pay your bills annually instead of monthly, as it works out cheaper.
5. Make necessary adjustments as and when items in your budget change.

6. Understand the difference berween needs and wants.
7. Monitor your progress
8. Look for 0% financial products that have the best extended periods (i.e. a 0% credit card that gives you 36 months or more to pay it off). You can then save your money to make overpayments on loans and debts (as discussed in chapter three).
9. When you have accumulated some disposable income (as discussed in chapter three). Start budgeting for financial goals like savings and investments, emergencies, annual bills, holidays and big purchases (such as a car).
10. Give yourself a little reward when you have established a functional budget that is working (this may take a few months).

Keep going I promise you it will get easier. If you have a month that you are not happy with that is ok. Temporary setbacks are all part of the journey, use that setback as a stepping stone to get back on track.

All this is possible if you can stick to a budget and manage it to the best of your ability. You will become savvy in budgeting because you will be budgeting the smart way!

Ask yourself the following questions:

1. Should I start budgeting right away?
2. Can I sort out my finances without a budget?
3. Are my finances too messed up to budget?
4. Do I need some help to start budgeting?
5. Am I budgeting the smart way?

TIP

Budgeting is such a powerful tool. The fundamental rule in this part of the game is having a highly detailed budget. The more detailed your budget, meaning it lists absolutely everything coming in and going out, the more control you will have of your finances. Try using one of the budgeting tools I suggested. I never leave home without mine!

Chapter 7

Having an Idea Can Make
You a Millionaire!

Being Creative Can Make You Rich

In this chapter, we will look at other ways to make money and maximise it. You will learn in this chapter how you can take the simplest idea and become a millionaire. It is time to start thinking outside the box. It is your financial 'game plan,' so you can tailor it to benefit you.

We all have gifts and talents that we may not have tapped into; I will let you into a little secret. Gifts and talents usually come from within, so you do not have to go to the ends of the earth to find them. They are already there.

Taking the first step to making things happen can seem quite daunting. Dreaming big and visualising is a good place to begin. We all have to start somewhere. Your dreams may influence how big you think, thus resulting in what you can make happen. I am continually dreaming and forever thinking big. This is what you will need to do to tap into any creative abilities you may have.

In challenging financial times like this, people will need an eye for opportunities and seize the moment to try and create wealth. Take the great depression in 1944. Out of that economic crisis, Wall Street was born, and it has been one of the worlds' financial power districts ever since.

People need multiple sources of income to be somewhat financially safe. It has been suggested that the minimum sources of income should be three. You may be thinking where on earth would I get three sources of income from?

You may be surprised at what you find when you start searching these out. The three sources of income that I am continuously building on albeit it is a work in progress are:

1. My business
2. My Properties
3. My book

"Nothing is more beautiful and romantic than when provision and purpose kiss." – Pastor Matthew Ashimolow

How I got started

People have always asked me how I manage my money so well. They are curious about the way I stretch it to do the things I have done for my family and me. This question has been asked more and more frequently over the years, to the point that each time I was asked the question, it began to trigger various thoughts.

These thoughts became clearer as time went by, it was apparent that these people really wanted answers. They were looking for help and support to manage and maximise their finances but were uncertain as to where or how to find it.

Years went by and I did nothing about this until one of my friends invited me to a womens' millionaires Bootcamp conference. The guest speakers were all millionaires who basically explained how they became millionaires and how you could become one too. They were being paid a large amount of money to speak for 90 minutes. When I heard that, I thought I could do what they were doing.

Without further ado, I made a beeline for one of the speakers, and I was fortunate to get the opportunity to speak to her. I told her what I would like to do – have my own conference explaining how I manage and maximise my money. I am aware that I talk quite a lot, so I decided to use it to my advantage and see this as one of my gifts or talents. My family may say I talk too much, but let us not go there right now!

The speaker advised me to get a few friends together, about five to ten, find a church hall or something similar and start that way.

Shortly after that conference, I met my friend Shelley for coffee. She too asked me the same questions about how I managed my money so well. Again, as always, I began to explain this to her, but there was clearly not enough time, and it would take longer than a lunch hour. After I left my friend, I went back to my office and said to my colleague that it was time for me to have my first money management conference. I finally took the step of faith and did it. As I have previously mentioned, I always think big – so my so-called church hall was a hotel in the city of London with the attendance of 40 delegates.

What did I learn in this process of taking the first step?

From the quote taken from the Motivational Speaker Les Brown, my learning was this: *"When* you do not know what your limits are, you can go as high as you want."* I was not sure how to pursue the gift that was within me. I knew I had something positive to share, but my big question was, 'But how?' Finally, I stepped out in faith and confidence, not sure what to expect, and I have not looked back. I have gone from strength to strength!

As Erik Weihenmayer, the first blind man to climb Mount Everest, said, "You cannot have self-confidence without some real skills that enable you to be successful."

She's Got Talent

A few years ago, a colleague that I previously worked with told me about a woman who worked in an interior design shop. She was known for creating beautiful displays for the home – bingo! Like myself, this woman had obviously been asked on many occasions how she did what she did. It got to a point whereby she became so inundated with enquiries that she felt the prompting to use her creativity and initiative to make something happen.

Therefore, she began profiling her customers. I want to highlight how important it is to do as much research as possible on your subject matter. This will help you give it your best shot when stepping out to do something new. Whatever area of work you are going into, knowing the client group/audience you are targeting is imperative. Another key factor that will determine whether you are successful or not; is to remember that proper preparation prevents poor performance. Well, all I can say is, this savvy woman prepared very well, to the point that she may have identified a new source of income.

She researched her customers' profiles which outlined their profession, salary bracket, house price bracket, where they shopped (i.e. Waitrose, Marks & Spencers) and so forth. On the back of that information, she tailored quality products to suit her customers. She took the step and opened up her house to show people how to decorate their home for Christmas.

The programme for the day included a light lunch and refreshments, all for the amount of wait for it - £120. I could not believe it, and I am sure some of you are thinking the same thing. As I am writing this, it only costs £24 to get into Buckingham Palace. What a shrewd woman! The truth of the matter is, she values what she does, and it was evident that her customers felt the same.

I have two things to say about this. Firstly, when you are confident about your goods and services and there is a demand, you will know what money you can command. Secondly, for that kind of money, all I can say is, a light lunch would definitely not be sufficient for many people like myself. For that kind of money, we would want an all-day buffet serving jerk chicken, rice and peas, and Guinness punch – and that is just part of the menu!

Remember I talked about researching well in the area you wish to step out in? This woman did a great job; she knew she could command that kind of money from the research she had done because she knew her clientele. Her capacity for each setting was ten people, the response was much more than she expected, to the point that she had to open her house up over three days! What a tidy sum she must have made.

She has possibly created another source of income doing what she loves and has a passion for. One of the most beautiful things in life is doing something you are passionate about and being paid for it. I am sure this is something that many people dream about. To top it off, it probably does not seem like work at all. Working smart and not too hard (if possible) who would not want that?

Now I have given you some food for thought, what ideas do you have in the back of your mind, in the back of a drawer somewhere on a scrap pad? It is time to seek them out so you can start working on them to make yourself some money. Give it some thought, have you been passionate about something for years but not explored it yet?

I am so enthusiastic about helping people discover and maximise their potential. I have worked with clients of all ages from as young as five, and I have found that there is something of substance in everyone. You may think you have no idea right now, but I am telling you it is there. It just might need some exploring to bring it out. We all have a purpose, whether it is to change lives, solve a problem or make a difference.

From conception to birth

I never thought I could ever write a book. (I guess it is another one of my hidden talents.) While writing this book, it has been such an interesting journey and experience. The only way I can describe this experience is that it seemed very similar to when I was expecting a baby.

In the beginning, I was excited and overjoyed. Then with each trimester came its own highs and lows, such as feeling the first kick, (a high) the horror of seeing the first stretch mark (a low). There were times when my thoughts flowed, and I was able to write with ease (a high) and other times I had no thoughts whatsoever (a low). There were periods when I felt physically and mentally drained. These rollercoaster thoughts and feelings were becoming increasingly identical to when I was expecting a baby. The one thought that stood out for me when I was pregnant, was, there is no turning back I had to keep going, similarly, I knew I had written too much to stop now!

By the time I got to the last 'trimester' (the proofreading and editing, it became quite intense). I was ready to deliver this book. My thoughts at this point were, "Never again; I am never writing another book."

Doesn't this sound very similar to a woman in labour? During labour, many thoughts and feelings are raging in a woman's mind and body. One of the most common thoughts women have is, 'I am never going through this again.' That is exactly what I kept saying to myself and other people.

However, when a mother sees her bundle of joy for the first time, all those thoughts and feelings go out the window. And that is exactly what I am sure to experience when I finished writing this book.

The joy in my heart, a sense of relief as well as being very overwhelmed by this accomplishment. I feel certain that I will not be able to find the words to explain these wonderful emotions. More often than not, once a mother has her baby, she will go on to have other children. Who knows, this may be the case for me with the possibility of another book!

The reason I shared this analogy with you is that once again I want to encourage and empower you to believe that 'having an idea can make you a millionaire'.

What have you taken from this chapter? Try answering the following questions?

1. Ask yourself, do you have any gifts or talents?
2. What are your reoccurring dreams/visions?
3. What are you passionate about?
4. Do you have any ideas that can make you a pretty penny?
5. Would you dare to take the first step to actualise your dream?

TIP

Take a few moments to think about things you do well without giving it much thought. It may be something you are passionate about but have never seen it as a gift or a talent. This could be your trump card in this game. Remember, it just takes one 'idea' to create wealth and make you a millionaire.

Chapter 8

Now Start Setting Your Goals

In this final chapter, I hope you will agree that this is where all the action really begins. I am optimistic that by now, you have attempted to unclutter some of your mind. The faulty perceptions, attitudes and beliefs about managing your money should have somewhat shifted. In other words, some things will now have to be learnt, unlearnt and relearnt. Let's take a look at each stage, it's definitions and their benefits.

Things to Learn:

Knowledge and skills, such as the following:

1. Understanding banks' basic principles and applying them to your finances (as discussed throughout this book).

2. How to budget.
3. How to set specific financial goals, i.e. how much you want to save or pay on a particular debt and when (set dates).
4. How to be accountable to someone, a friend or family member to help keep you on track.

Things to Unlearn:

Some of your spending habits, such as the following:

1. Overspending – giving in to your urge or emotions despite the consequences.
2. Impulse spending – a lack of self-control/emotions.
3. The latest trend spending – keeping up with the Joneses.
4. Entitlement spending – instant gratification.

Things to Relearn:

Self-discipline, such as the following:

1. How to save for what you want or need instead of purchasing it on credit.

2. Be mindful of spending more than you have coming in.
3. Stop what you are doing; go over the rules in this game to prevent further debt.
4. Ask for help. We all need help at some point in our lives – it is ok to ask for it.

Some of these points may have caused you to have a house full of unwanted or unnecessary things that total a tidy sum. Reflecting on this may well help you conclude that this tidy sum has contributed to the financial situation you are in today.

The good news is, in this book, you have been given insight into what may have caused some of the mindsets you currently have. This newfound knowledge can assist you in making the necessary changes to get your thinking on the right track. If you carefully take a look at these actions, you will notice that quite a few of them start with your mindset - interesting!

Here are some things you may want to consider if you are not sure where to start. Understanding and mastering the basic principles is essential for making the right financial choices. The ultimate goal is to become financially literate. The first steps to becoming financially literate are as follows:

1. Read and Research as Much as You Can

Whatever financial product you need, make sure you research, research, and research again. When informed decisions need to be made, especially those that can affect you and your entire family. Ask yourself:

- Is it right for me or us?
- Do I really need it?
- Can I afford it?
- What if my circumstances change?

There can be various outcomes, so you need to thoroughly explore and research the situation to minimise any unexpected consequences.

Your decision making also requires that you assess your attitude toward risks. To do this, you may need assistance from a Financial Advisor. As previously discussed in an earlier chapter, life can be full of uncertainty. Spending time to examine the risk will act as a valuable measure to take and contribute to the financial decisions you make. This goes back to educating yourself about finance. The more knowledge you have about a subject matter, the better informed your decisions will always be.

2. Network with People Inside and Outside Your Circle

Are there some people you know who seem to be financially secure and have a good quality of life? See if you can arrange some time with them to find out what they are doing. Enquire into what has worked well for them to stay ahead of the game financially. They may also be able to advise you of any pitfalls they have experienced.

You can also seek a financial expert such as an Independent Financial Advisor or someone from the Citizens Advice Bureau etc. They will look at your circumstances to assess how you are managing your finances.

If required they will assist you in looking at a workable strategy to pay off your debts, contact creditors on your behalf, and help with putting a freeze on the interest on some of your debts. They can also consolidate your debts to manage your finances better, to achieve some financial stability.

3. Use Financial Management Tools

There is no excuse anymore as previously mentioned. There are some fantastic online free apps (the information is in the appendix at the back of the book). They are out there for you to download they can do the following:

1. Track your finances.
2. See what areas you are spending in.
3. Give you prompts to pay your bills (if they are not paid by direct debit).
4. Connect your bank accounts to view what is coming in.
5. Set saving goals
6. Update you on any current changes, such as interest rates, bank charges etc.
7. Inform you of other activities that are going on in the bank that may affect your accounts.

4. Good Debt, Bad Debt

Debt is something that affects eight out of ten people. So, debt is something we all need to pay attention to. Therefore, understanding the difference between good debt and bad debt will help you become financially stable.

Good debt is borrowing money for assets or investments i.e. a mortgage, investment properties or a product that will generate a long-term income.

Bad debt is using credit with high-interest rates to purchase cars, clothes, holidays and a lifestyle you truly cannot afford. One where you have not really planned for or does not fit within your budget because what you have going out is far more then what you have coming in.

5. Think Smart Plan For the Future

1. Where do you see yourself financially or would like to see yourself in the next one to five years?
2. How do you think you will get there?
3. What are some of the ways you think you can make this happen?
4. Your attitude will mostly influence this - remember the power of the mind.

Take a few moments to think about these questions. See how many you can answer. Why not write them down in a book and record the day you wrote them? This will be a point of reference for you that you can revisit regularly.

I would suggest that each time you revisit these questions you write down any thoughts or actions you have taken and date it. This is called journaling. I often use this intervention with my clients in therapy. It acts as a powerful tool because you have documented what is taking place and when. Seeing where you were when you started this journey and where you are now can be a great way to motivate yourself.

On the other hand, if you have not done as well as you would have expected, it can still be used as a tool to help you reflect on what you need to do. Your documented answers can give you a good indication of where you are in this game and the possible next step to take.

Becoming Financially Free

Working toward financial freedom means putting things in place to try and make that happen.

As I have mentioned continuously throughout this book, this starts with assessing your outgoings and looking at ways to reduce them. Once this starts to happen, you will then be in an excellent position to free up some money to create a disposable income.

Let us recap on how you can do this:

1. Pay your mortgage off earlier than the agreed contractual date (as discussed in chapter three).
2. Create a workable plan: pay off one regular outgoing/debt then work on the next one (as discussed in chapter three).
3. Look for better savings accounts with higher interest rates through comparison websites.
4. Use separate accounts for each financial goal if possible. I have banked with a particular bank for years, I have several accounts with them, some of which I am not using. Now that I have financial goals, they come in handy because I use each one for different goals. You too may have some accounts that you can use in the same way.

5. Invest your money in things like shares, property and investments funds etc. You should seek professional advice before making any investment decisions.

My final analogy

Life is a journey; in any journey, you need to have a destination in mind and a plan of how you intend to get there. Where has your financial journey taken you so far? Is it to a place called *pleasure* or a place called *pain*?

Whatever place you are in today, whether it was planned or not, the absence of setting some goals; i.e. having some form of savings or living within your means. Has determined if your journey has been a smooth sailing dream or a rough nightmare.

Goal setting is such an integral component in this game. Your goals will need to be implemented every step of the way to have success and be a winner. The difference between setting financial goals and not setting them is likened to getting on a plane and not knowing its destination. How would you know when you arrive? Some flights are not direct, and they may stop a couple of times. Ask yourself, will you be happy with where you end up?

In this book, I have attempted to give you a comprehensive overview of how best to manage your money. Your mindset is key, and that is why very early on in this book, I have given you some insight from a psychological perspective. Your mind is where you win or lose in this 'money management game'.

Knowing the banks' rules and playing by them, coupled with implementing the Three S's Strategy + Structure = Success - is paramount in winning in this game.

Next, I introduced you to five golden nuggets that will educate you financially for life. I encourage you to try these out. I have given examples as well as shared my own experiences. I hope I have clearly shown you how 'thinking like a bank' can save you thousands of pounds. Just by changing some of your regular financial practices you will be equipped to make savvy financial choices.

For example, if you begin to make fortnightly mortgage payments, it basically means that you do not have to add one penny to your monthly repayments. You simply change the way you pay it, and BOOM! You will be able to save thousands of pounds over the years.

For people who do not have a mortgage, there are other nuggets in the book that will work for you. Remember, you are never too young or too old to start learning how best to manage your money. Whether you start at the age of six or sixty, in this world we all need money to live, so age is irrelevant.

Managing money is a skill that needs to be mastered, first in your mind, secondly by knowing the rules. Thinking right and making some smart changes, will give you the power over your money. Once this happens you can begin to experience the quality of life you very much deserve.

It is time to start making your money work for you as opposed to you working for your money. When your money begins working for you, especially from various sources, you are on your way to reaching the ultimate goal of becoming financially stable and secure!

I hope that by the time you have got to this chapter and read it, you will be equipped to 'start setting your goals'.

That first step will have to be taken, whatever your situation may be. I took mine despite being apprehensive about the odds that were stacked up against me; it got the ball rolling, and I have never looked back!

I feel it is time to share my final story; there are two reasons I am passionate to share it with you. Firstly, to show you how much I believe that all things are possible if only you believe. Secondly, this is my last opportunity to attempt to empower and encourage you to start thinking differently.

Dreams Do Come True

One of my goals was to work toward having a more comfortable life where I did not have to work so hard. I wanted to live in the sun for half of the year.

What did I do to achieve this long-term goal?

As I mentioned earlier in the book that at the age of 21, I brought my first property, I sold it 14 years later. I kept my endowment policy going for a further 11 years as a form of saving/investment instead of cashing it in.

An endowment policy is a life insurance contract designed to pay a lump sum on the maturity of a product such as a mortgage or a loan. When I took out my mortgage for 25 years, I also took out an endowment policy for 25 years that would pay out a lump sum at the end of its term. It also covered me for death or any critical illness.

At the end of the 25-year term my endowment policy matured, so I now had money to do whatever I wished. For me, this meant I had a 'good seed' to plant. I thought about the best ways of planting it, and plant it I did!

Before the maturity of my endowment policy, I began to visualise my dream; a lovely detached house in Florida. Florida is only one hour and twenty minutes away from Jamaica by plane (that is almost the equivalent travel time of going to France from London).

I chose America because I travel to the States regularly and thought it would be a good investment. I ensured that I did my research carefully, and when I felt it was economically beneficial to buy a house, bingo, it was bought! A word of caution; never be hasty when buying something of value, especially when it involves a large sum of money like buying a house. ***Hasty decisions make for bad decisions.***

I did not want a financial burden, so I thoroughly researched the prospects of buying and renting in America. I looked at everything from the rental income for that particular area, to the ins and outs of housing associations. I found out that each state, as well as different areas within that state, have different policies. The point I am highlighting here is, a lot of research had to be done so that an informed decision could be made.

From the time I purchased my house, it has been rented out on a yearly lease which means it has been paying for itself. At some point, the plan is to borrow some money from that property and purchase another house in the states. Again the strategy here is to use some of the rental income from that property to help towards the new property. Back in chapter five, I share this same strategy that my dad used – history repeating itself! This is how you begin to build wealth, what is happening here is I am starting to accumulate assets to build my property portfolio.

I understand that you may not have an Endowment policy to invest, but at some point, in time if you follow the rules in this game, you may well have something. If you are in a position where your finances are unstable at the moment, then one of your priority goals should be to start working on a plan to take control of your finances (this starts with having a detailed budget.) Nothing can begin to happen until your finances are in order. I cannot emphasise enough that it is achievable if you really want it.

If I did not have a resourceful attitude about money,

I probably would not be in the position I am in today. At the time I sold my first property I was a single mother with three young children. It would have been so easy for me to cash in my endowment policy and taken the money and splashed it all. But I didn't.

I always had big dreams that I constantly visualised. I saw myself sitting around a pool sipping cocktails in the sun. Isn't that enough to keep you dreaming? I can now testify that dreams do come true! I have encouraged my children to think big also, and now their dreams seem bigger than mine. So, my advice to you here is, dare to dream! Einstein once said, "Dreams are the future that is to come true."

I am showing you that once you learn the necessary skills and techniques of maximising your money. Whether you are single, a single parent, married, have lots of money or a little money, your money can be maximised. I hope you are getting the picture. Think about it!

Are You Courageous Enough?

Courage is the act of taking a step despite your fear. I genuinely understand that changing your way of thinking can cause various anxieties about different things. One of the biggest challenges that it highlights is the impact it has on our mind, which affects our emotional state.

The emotional state I am referring to here is one of the most powerful emotions of them all and that is fear. The fear of failing, fear of disappointment or embarrassment, the fear of peoples' thoughts or opinions, the list goes on and on. For this reason, many people remain stuck, frustrated, and hopeless.

I want this book to be instrumental in helping you overcome any obstacle that is preventing you from becoming your own Personal Money Management Advisor (PMMA). With that said, my final plan of action to help you accomplish this is to leave you with some positive quotes from influential people; this may just be what you need to help you get started!

Positive Mindset:

1. "A man is not the orchestrator of his life; he is the orchestrator of his mindset. The quality and quantity of his success are dependent on the latter." *Chelsea Murray-Clarke*
2. "Be a yardstick of quality. Some people aren't used to an environment where excellence is expected." *– Steve Jobs*
3. "My mission in life is not merely to survive, but to thrive; and to do so with some passion, some compassion, some humour, and some style." *– Maya Angelou*
4. "Our greatest weakness lies in giving up. The most certain way to succeed is always to try just one more time." *– Thomas Edison*
5. "The secret of getting ahead is getting started." *– Mark Twain*

Courage:

1. "Man can live about forty days without food, about three days without water, about eight minutes without air, but only for one second without hope." *– Hal Lindsey*

2. *"True strength is keeping everything together when everyone expects you to fall apart." – **Unknown***
3. *"*Strength does not come from winning. Your struggles develop your strengths. When you go through hardships and decide not to surrender, that is a strength." – ***Arnold Schwarzenegger***
4. *"*Success is not final, failure is not fatal: it is the courage to continue that counts." – ***Winston Churchill***
5. "All our dreams can come true if we have the courage to pursue them." – ***Walt Disney***

Acknowledgements

First and foremost, I would like to thank God for the grace, wisdom and knowledge he has given me to write this book. I am also grateful for all the kind assistance and support I received to help get this book out there and into the hands of everyone that needs to become financially savvy.

I want to thank my children Adrian, Chelsea and Nicole for helping me put my money management knowledge and experience into practice during the season in my life of being a single mother. That surely was a time of financial trials and testing. I can fully acknowledge that the journey I have been on with my children has played an integral part in me becoming financially savvy and debt- free.

Special thanks go out to Stella Akinsiku who has assisted me with this project throughout. Stella has also given me valuable and insightful suggestions and feedback every step of the way.

Much appreciation goes out to a special friend that read my very first draft and helped me make sense of it, as well as develop its structure.

Finally, I would like to express my gratitude to my dear friends and family that believed in my vision for writing this book. Your encouragement has been empowering and motivating.

Thank you all so very much.

To The Reader

My hope is that this book has inspired, empowered and made you stop and think about taking the first step to maximise and manage your money. Although written in the UK, its principles can be applied worldwide. Throughout the book I teach, coach, counsel, and mentor. The content is dynamic and life-changing; this book is designed to help you start living the financial abundant life you so deserve

Being in the know

I feel confident that I have given you enough information and knowledge about financial institutions practices. Whether you are applying their principals to benefit you or making savvy financial choices, guess what? You are *Thinking Like a Bank*.

I am optimistic that my candid transparent approach has capitulated the attention of my readers. I share some of my valley experiences of living on the breadline with three small children, barely making ends meet, to working my way up the mountain and possessing a property portfolio.

Dreams do come true

Why not ask yourself the following questions:

- ➢ Do you have any dreams?
- ➢ If you do what are they?
- ➢ How can you make your dream become a reality?
- ➢ If you don't have a dream, I invite you to start dreaming from today.

Hopefully, there is something in this book for everyone to help kick start your dreams to make them come true.

Money is a fundamental part of life, it influences most things we desire to do or have. *Thinking like a bank* is where people that have money start from, so why don't you?

Finally, I will leave you with one last famous quote from Pastor Matthew Ashimolowo that I feel sums up this book. It goes like this - "If it's going to be, it's up to me".

Appendix

Banks functions, *5*
Becoming financially free, *133*

Budgeting, *103*
Budgeting the smart way, *111*
How to budget, *104*
The purpose of budgeting, *104*
Why you should budget, *109*

Credit, *16*

Debt, *55*
Compounded interest for debt, *56*
Fixed debt, *58*
Good debt/bad debt, *131*
Psychology of debt, *37*
Revolving debt, *56*

Disposable income, *31*

Endowment policy, *139*
Financial Products, *65*

Mortgage payments, *68*

Payment Protection Insurance (PPI), *77*

Savings, *28*
Compounded interest for savings, *38*
Savvy savings, *28*

Start setting your goals, *126*

Useful Websites for Good Deals

Groupon groupon.com

LivingSocial livingsocial.com

Martin Lewis moneysavingexpert.com

Travelzoo top20ukdeals@email.travelzoo.com

Weekly shopping deals mysupermarket.co.uk

savethestudent.org/ moneywise.co.uk / lovemoney.com

www.mirror.co.uk

Comparison Websites

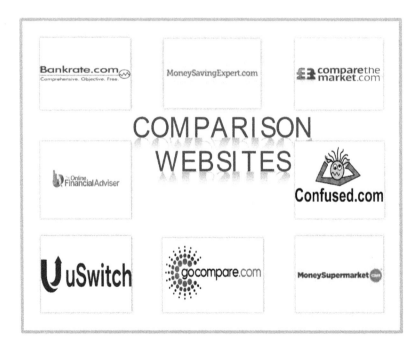

Free Banking Apps

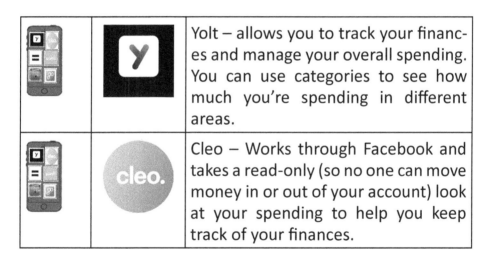

	y	Yolt – allows you to track your finances and manage your overall spending. You can use categories to see how much you're spending in different areas.
	cleo.	Cleo – Works through Facebook and takes a read-only (so no one can move money in or out of your account) look at your spending to help you keep track of your finances.

		Money Dashboard – Categorises your spending and displays all incoming and outgoing amounts on a dashboard chart, so you can see what you have spent in different areas
	pariti	Pariti – Connects you bank accounts: you can view what you have coming in plus set spending goals. It updates automatically each day so you can see what you've left to spend.
		Spending Tracker – You can choose to track your spending weekly, monthly or yearly.
	go	goHenry – Helps parents teach their children aged 6-18 how to save, spend and budget.

Consultation

What I offer: 6 weeks of one-on-one sessions on a weekly, fortnightly or monthly basis.

How you can benefit: A tailored strategy to manage and maximise your money.

My Contact details

Norma Cassius

T: 07845891035

E: nc@normacassius.com.

W: www.normacassius.com